THE BOND OF BLUE

Written by
Mary Pierre Quinn-Stanbro
&
Michele Graves

NFB Publishing
Buffalo, NY

Printed in the United States of America

The Bond of Blue/ Quinn-Stanbro & Graves 1st Edition

ISBN: 978-1-953610-32-4

1.Title 2. Police. 3. Family. 4. Buffalo, New York

Part 2 is a work of fiction. All characters are fictitious, unless specified, names have been changed when necessary. Any resemblance to actual events or locations, unless specified, or persons, living or dead is entirely coincidental.

Cover design and photo editing by Doreen Boyer DeBoth

NFB
NFB Publishing/Amelia Press
119 Dorchester Road
Buffalo, New York 14213

For more information visit Nfbpublishing.com

DEDICATION

This story is dedicated to my family members who have served or are serving in law enforcement, and all the men and women who have served or are serving on the Buffalo Police Department.

Thank you for your service and for taking the Oath.

The Buffalo Police Department Oath:

I do solemnly swear that I will support the Constitution of the United States and the Constitution of the State of New York and that I will faithfully discharge the duties of the office of (position) in the Police Department of the City of Buffalo to the best of my ability.

ACKNOWLEDGEMENTS

Maryellen Thirolf (my father's sister), for the photos of her father, Frank P. Quinn, and the articles from their family's scrapbook from the *Buffalo News* and the *Courier- Express* showcasing his years on the Buffalo Police Department.

Chief Dennis J. Richards, Buffalo Police Department

Lt. G. Rak, Buffalo Police Department, Retired

Mark Lemke, North Tonawanda Police Department, Retired

Richard A. Shear, formerly with LA County Sheriff's Department

John Arnone

James Banko

Mary Grace Battaglia

Julie Quinn Blyth

Mary Ann Moriarity

Amelia O'Connor

Peggy Novara

Gene Stanbro

A portion of the proceeds from this book will go to the St. Joseph Collegiate Institute Aaron Graves Memorial Scholarship

TABLE OF CONTENTS

PART 1

PART 2

Author's Note

Part 1 is a true story and references newspaper articles regarding cases from 1939–1962 involving Officer Frank P. Quinn.

Part 2 is a supplemental work of fiction based on an actual case mentioned in part 1.

PART 1

PREFACE

In 2016, my dad, Francis "Butch" P. Quinn passed away. It was devastating to all ten of us children and his wife. My dad was a Buffalo Police Officer for 31 years. He retired in 1997. I remember growing up feeling especially privileged and so proud of the fact that my dad was a Buffalo Police Officer. I wish I had learned more of his stories about his years on the force or any of the stories his father may have passed down to him from his years as a police officer. My grandfather, Frank P. Quinn, was with the Buffalo Police Department (BPD) for 23 years.

Growing up as the daughter of a police officer, I came to understand police officers are a rare breed. They leave their home and family and go out into an unforgiving world, where it is their responsibility to make it a safer place for people they do not even know. Each day they put on their police uniform and badge and pack their gun. They control crowds, keep order, and perform many tasks that most of us would rather not do—all while not knowing if they will make it back safely to their families at the end of their shift. It is a profession that is not always looked upon in a favorable light, but these brave men and women have my respect and admiration.

If you were to look at the Buffalo NY Police Patch, you would see a ship on the water heading towards a lighthouse. I see my Dad and grandfather as representing the beacons of light on that patch. The definition of a beacon is someone or something that guides or gives hope to others; that is what I believe Francis P. Quinn and Frank P. Quinn accomplished during their combined 54 years with the BPD. Although I chose not to pursue the profession of a police officer, I still felt compelled to contribute to my family's legacy to protect and serve in my own way. While I was not qualified to protect, I was able to serve. Being actively involved in various community endeavors in the City of Buffalo, I was invited to join the Buffalo Police Commissioner's Citizen's Advisory Group (CAG). I served under four Police Commissioners for over twenty years as the Recording Secretary for the CAG. The CAG was comprised of citizens from neighborhood groups, faith based, business based and community based organizations. They were appointed to the CAG by their respective groups so that they were not perceived as a "rubber stamp" for the Buffalo Police Department. They provided a much needed information conduit between the community and the Police Commissioner. This involvement gave me a strong sense of connection to the *bond of blue*, the indescribable union between all those serving in law enforcement. I was part of the common thread that then entwined me with my father and grandfather, even if only in a small way.

I wrote this work from my heart to honor my father. The main story is a non-fictional account of his life through my eyes, using my voice. It begins with his father's life (my grandfather) and his career with the BPD, which is where I believe it all started. My grandfather passed away before he was able to see his son join the BPD, but their *bond of blue* could not be broken even through death. This story showcases their dedication to the BPD and, more importantly, to our families. While their chosen profession was very important to both of them, *family above all* took precedence in their lives and it is what they will be most remembered for. The story takes the reader through my dad's childhood, his career with the BPD, and the life he had with my mother, our family, and me. It then spans through to his death and beyond.

There is an axiom that I have come to believe: "I am me because of the reflection I see of you." I feel it was because of my dad's strong work ethic and his "never give up" attitude that I was driven to put this story in writing; perhaps my dad was what he was because of his father's reflection.

Since I didn't have much information regarding my dad's upbringing or my grandfather, I reached out to my dad's sister, Maryellen; his best friend growing up named Jim, and my Uncle Richard. They were able to share stories with me about my dad. Also, I contacted his former partner on the BPD's Tactical Patrol Unit. He also shared stories with me that were uplifting and heart wrenching.

At the end of the memoir is a fictional, supplemental story about the death of an infant child I named "Danny Boy." It incorporates one of the newspaper articles I received regarding an actual case my grandfather worked on involving the murder of a baby boy back in 1946. Since my grandfather was such a family man, I believe this case must have affected him deeply.

I learned from communications with Dad's family and friends that even when he was young, music was a very important part of his life. His music was a constant presence in the background of our lives as we grew up, so I had firsthand knowledge of the artists he loved. Our family dynamics revolved around including his music choices at every gathering. This story is told using the songs he would listen to or were relevant to that period of time. Therefore, it is truly a poignant playlist of his life.

PROLOGUE

IT WAS ANOTHER Saturday evening in 2015 when our Quinn clan—including siblings, spouses, and children—all gathered for our weekly family bonding session featuring food, drinks, and music. These evenings were so special to us. With each passing year, our dinner table would have another one or two new participants. One of us would have either married or had a child, and sometimes friends and neighbors just asked if they could join in on these amazing times. I called our weekly gatherings "The Last Supper." It may sound morbid, but Dad would tell us that with every passing day, hour, or minute, you never knew when your time on earth would be over. He wanted to live week to week with us and share those times as if it were our last with all of us together. I didn't see it as a sad thing, but rather an honor and privilege that we had all survived another week and were able to get together to share in the libations and be in the presence of Dad.

On this particular occasion, we learned that Dad had gone for tests due to a cough he just could not shake. He explained to us with his characteristic nonchalance that he would be starting treatment the following week for lung cancer. That night's festivities were bittersweet. We hung on every word Dad said and we did not want him to stop talking. I remember wondering why we had never asked him the questions we were asking that night. We were starving for his knowledge of current events, baseball, and his time with the BPD. Perhaps it was because he was a man of few words; while he loved to sit around the table and listen to all of our chatter, he preferred to sit back and take it all in. He didn't talk just to talk. If he had something to say, it must have been important to him; or else he wouldn't have said it.

Dad didn't start with his room temperature Budweiser but went right to his Southern Comfort on the rocks. From that point on, he started to open up to us about his life. Or perhaps we just really began to listen. Since I am the oldest of the ten Quinn children, I felt it was my honor to share Dad's story. As I said, he was a man of few words, so I am telling his story for him.

Most families have something that unifies them as they go through their lives. It could be a prayer, a saying, a joke, or a song. For us, the children of Francis P. Quinn, it was and still is:

"An Olde Irish Toast"

May you be in heaven an hour before the devil knows you're dead.

Dead you're knows

Devil the before

Hour an

Heaven in

Be you May

Toast Irish Olde An

This toast is very important to our family. Every one of us knows the words forward and backward. As I drove home that evening thinking about Dad and his upcoming battle, it occurred to me the words to the toast might be foreshadowing the future. Tears streamed down my face as I prayed to God to not let our dad die. Please give us a few more years with him.

MAY YOU
BE IN
Heaven
AN HOUR
BEFORE THE
DEVIL
KNOWS YOU'RE
DEAD

WHEN IRISH EYES ARE SMILING

My grandfather, Frank P. Quinn, was born in 1914 to Irish immigrants. After arriving in the U.S., they settled into the First Ward section of Buffalo, New York on Vincennes Street. They had four daughters and four sons. Frank's brother, John P. Quinn, was the Captain of Precinct 15, the South Park Station of the Buffalo Police Department. John was ten years older than Frank, and Frank completely idolized his big brother. The desire to protect and serve ran in their family. In 1939 Frank was appointed to the Buffalo Police Department as a Patrolman.

In 1940, Frank married a young woman named Julia (my grandmother). He and Julia were the proud parents of four beautiful children: William (Bill), Francis (Butch) my dad, Maryellen, and Thomas (Thom). Their family lived in the first floor flat of a two-family home on Pries Avenue in a house owned by Julia's mother.

Julia was very proud of her husband becoming a police officer, though they did not have much money on Frank's starting salary as a BPD Patrolman. To supplement their income, he and Julia both worked part-time at the same post office. She was a mail sorter, and he was a clerk.

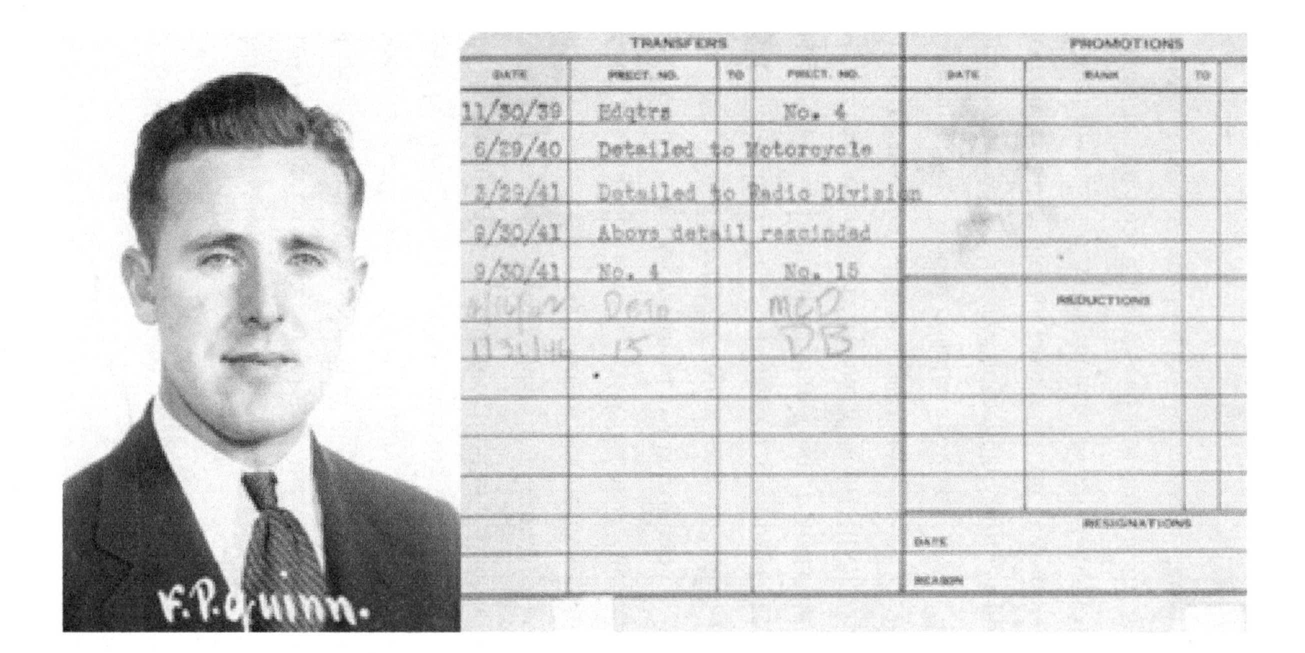

TRANSFERS			
DATE	PRECT. NO.	TO	PRECT. NO.
11/30/39	Hdqtrs		No. 4
6/29/40	Detailed to Motorcycle		
3/29/41	Detailed to Radio Division		
9/30/41	Above detail rescinded		
9/30/41	No. 4		No. 15
[illegible]	Dets		MCD
[illegible]	15		DB

PROMOTIONS		
DATE	RANK	TO

REDUCTIONS

RESIGNATIONS

DATE

REASON

Frank encouraged his three sons to be involved in sports, especially baseball. That is how their Sundays would be shared as a family. The family did not attend Sunday Mass together because all of his children were required to attend the Children's Mass at 9:00 am at Holy Family Church on South Park Avenue, where there were over 1,200 children in attendance. However, Frank attended daily mass at St. Joseph's Cathedral downtown which was close to Police Headquarters on Franklin Street. After the Children's Mass, the children would go home and have their special Sunday breakfast. Julia was of Ukrainian descent and she would make her family her famous *Paska* bread, eggs, Canadian bacon, and fried spam. After breakfast, she would have her children change out of their Sunday best, and they would head over to Mungovan Park. Other kids in the neighborhood would join them at the park and they would play ball until dinner time.

The end to their perfect day would be when they would all come together as a family and sit down to eat their Sunday dinner of roast beef with au jus gravy. As a special treat, Julia would bake an apple pie for dessert and put a chunk of Velveeta cheese on top of it for Frank. He would lead his family in a prayer of thanks before every meal. He was a religious man, but he connected to his faith in a private way. Beyond attending mass, meal prayers, and prayers on his knees before bed, he kept the rest of his religious convictions to himself.

There was one young lad in the neighborhood who was best friends with Dad, and his brother Bill. His name was Jim. Whenever the Quinn boys would play ball or card games in their basement, Jim was there with them. Although baseball seemed to occupy most of their time, they would also go and shoot baskets at the playground in Mulroy Park on Tifft Street in the winter until their hands were frozen. Dad, Bill, and Jim were inseparable, and would sometimes sneak out onto the roof of the garage behind the Quinn home. They would talk about things that young boys, and later young men, would discuss.

The Quinn children were involved in many school activities in their South Buffalo school. One thing they all loved was music. Some of their favorite artists were Pat Boone, Ricky Nelson, and Elvis Presley. They ruled the music that was being played in the Quinn home. However, at times, Frank was able to play some of his favorite Irish music. He loved the songs, "An Irish Lullaby" and "When Irish Eyes are Smiling." His favorite was "Danny Boy." The Quinns were a happy family. Wanting a proper upbringing and the best for his family, Frank encouraged his children to be involved in sports, do well in school, and attend church. He felt blessed to be living the ideal American life.

Frank and Julia always made sure that there were plenty of things for their children to do to keep them out of trouble. They were also devoted to their relationship. A perfect night out for them would be a Saturday evening at the Legion Post in Fort Erie, Canada, with a small group of couples that would regularly gather there. They would all bring snacks, have a couple of drinks, and play card games. There would be Christmas, birthday, and Halloween parties at the Post. They would all come up with different costumes each year—everyone, that is, except Julia. She would wear her Ukrainian outfit to every party she could. Frank would just beam when he was with her. They truly were a beautiful couple. They were also usually the most boisterous group at the Post, but everyone wanted to be part of their special little group.

Most of the people there knew Frank was a police officer, but on those nights, he was just a regular guy out with his friends. Frank's drink of choice was beer. He had a taste for it and that was all he drank. He loved to socialize with people and just have simple fun. He was an unpretentious man. He didn't need a big beautiful home or extravagant vacations; he just wanted to spend time with his family and friends. Frank realized the importance of friendship. He had a way of making people feel special. People just seemed to gravitate to him and his Irish grin.

He loved taking his family on vacation to Crystal Beach in Canada. Once, in the summer of 1955, they rented a cottage there for an entire month. Even when his vacation days ended, Frank would drive back and forth each day in his 1954 Chevy to be with his family during their extended stay. They had a wonderful time in Crystal Beach, playing at the beach during the day, and playing cards in the evenings. Frank taught all of his children how to play pinochle. Although the family also spent a couple of other vacations in Long Beach and Wasaga Beach in Canada, Crystal Beach was where they longed to go.

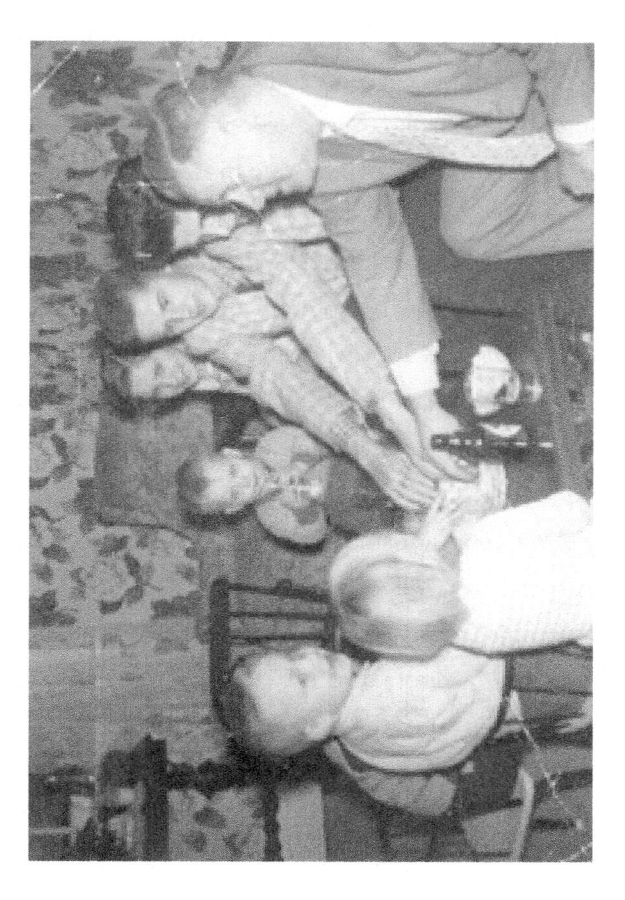

AS TIME GOES BY

FRANK WAS VERY busy with his home life and his career. After a couple of years on the BPD, he was appointed to Motorcycle Patrolman by the Police Commissioner. He was injured while on the job when his motorcycle skidded on some wet leaves. It wasn't a serious injury, thankfully, but the accident caused bruising on his arms and legs.

As Frank was moving up in the department, there were newspaper articles in *The Buffalo News* and *The Courier-Express* about how he would solve cases even when he was off duty or on vacation. One of those articles, published in 1945, was "Business Before Pleasure, Sleuth's Motto." [1] It congratulated Frank on letting business come before pleasure while he was enjoying his evening off sitting on his front porch. A man was visiting one of his neighbors a few doors down. When he came out to leave, he saw that his auto was not parked where he left it. The man recognized Frank sitting on the porch and asked him for help. Frank took the man in his own car and began looking for the missing vehicle. Within several minutes of driving around, they located the car around six blocks away with a 15-year old boy at the wheel! Case solved!

There was another newspaper article in 1945 about

Frank that stated that even while he was on vacation, he did a little investigating on his own. He picked up three boys in connection with the theft of a box of candy from a truck trailer in the parking lot of the Motor Express Corporation. Frank was driving south on Seneca Street when he saw the three boys. One of them appeared to be concealing something under his shirt, which piqued Frank's interest. The boy produced a box of candy and insisted that he found it. Frank told him to show him where he found it. The boys took him over to an area in the parking lot. When they arrived, there were two South Division Station Police cars with officers waiting. The boys had broken a seal on the door of one of the trailers. They were then turned over to the Youth Bureau.[2]

Just a year later, in 1946, there was one case that Frank was assigned to that probably affected him deeply. It was like any other day when he got a flash on his radio, alerting him that the body of a newborn baby had been found in a black cloth zipper bag on the ice of Scajaquada Creek near the West Avenue Bridge. The body was wrapped in the Sunday edition of a New York newspaper. There were a couple of kids playing on the ice of the creek bank who had made the discovery. One of the boys slid out on the ice and pulled the bag in, then called the police. Frank and his partner responded to the grim scene. They escorted the infant's body to the morgue.[3] Since Frank was such a family man, I believe the discovery and brutal murder of this little boy was something that stayed with him for the rest of his life.

Not long after that, in 1947, Frank was promoted to Acting Detective. Although he was not given permanent status as a detective at that time, he was given the salary of a detective while he was in that acting capacity. He was one of many police officers who were honored at the 58th Annual Police Ball in the Memorial Auditorium. There were nearly 8,000 people in attendance. Frank was one of thirteen officers cited for honorable mention.[4] He loved his home life and his career deeply, and was able to successfully manage both.

Frank's career really started to take off in 1949, and that was also when it changed forever. While he was an Acting Detective with the North Buffalo Squad, he became involved in the murder case of Floyd D. Chisholm, a liquor store owner on Fillmore Avenue in Buffalo. The police were baffled by an almost complete lack of clues until they identified Alfred Twarog as a potential suspect. Some witnesses supplied information that they saw Mr. Chisholm with a man shortly before his death, but other information did not match the description of Twarog.[5] Frank enmeshed himself in 24 hours of questioning the suspect, who was eventually charged with first-degree murder after a conference between Police Commissioner McMahon and the District Attorney's office.

Twarog had steadily denied any knowledge of the slaying, but Frank and the team kept up their interrogation and convinced the suspect that it would ease his mind if he told them the truth. It was then that he blurted out a confession and put it in writing, even reenacting the entire ordeal for Frank and the other officers. Utilizing simple old-fashioned police work, they were able to solve the case and Twarog was ultimately convicted. Newspaper articles even stated, "The Chisholm case is a warning that in Buffalo, nobody gets away with murder." [6]

Within a week of that article, Frank was presented with a letter from Peter J. Crotty of Chester C. Gorski's Office, 44th District, New York, Congress of the United States, House of Representatives, Washington, DC. The letter congratulated him for his part in solving the Chisholm murder case. It even went so far as to state, "I hope that the newspaper statement to the effect that you will soon be promoted is true and accurate. It certainly would be a promotion well merited."

The Chisholm case opened up doors for Frank. In 1950, he and his partner were honored by the Retail Liquor Stores Association of Western New York for their work in solving the murder of Floyd Chisholm. They were presented diamond rings set in onyx. The Association President said the gifts were the first of their kind in the history of the Association. Police Commissioner Noeppel stated, "Work of the two detectives reflects a great deal of credit for the Police Department and exemplified it in its true light."[7]

Following this case, Frank moved up the ranks of the BPD rather quickly. His family was so proud of him being mentioned regularly in the local papers. One article in particular was the family's favorite. A story in the spring of 1952 referenced an Easter Egg Hunt at the Buffalo Zoo, where three Quinn children had a lucky day. Two of them found prize-winning eggs and the third, Butch, had "found daddy", who had somehow vanished as the children left to hunt eggs.[8] He was a man with such a big heart and soul who truly loved the job and he truly loved his family.

Frank continued to advance and receive promotions

for the next several years. In 1954 Commissioner DeCillis promoted him to Detective. In 1955, he went to the North Side Squad (Auto) and was elevated to Detective Sergeant; he was then transferred to the Homicide Squad under Commissioner Cannan. In 1960, he was promoted to the head of the District A Squad.

While Frank's job with the BPD was going very well for him, the dynamics of his family life were changing. His oldest sons, Bill and Francis (Dad), had become young men. They were moving out of the family home on Pries Avenue to start their careers and families. Frank and Julia still had two younger children at home and they continued to enjoy their lives until the summer of 1962.

Unfortunately, that is when the Quinn family and the Buffalo community lost a father, husband, public servant, and friend. My grandfather passed away at home in his favorite chair. Earlier that summer he had been injured on the job. It was a knee injury and he was off on disability recovering at home. The doctors said that perhaps he passed away from a blood clot that traveled to his heart. Julia and the kids were beside themselves with grief, but with the support of Frank's friends on the BPD and Julia's fortitude to go on for her family, they got through the most difficult time of their lives.

ALL SHOOK UP

I FELT IT was important to begin my memoir by obtaining some background information on my grandfather. In doing so, I realized he and Dad shared many of the same strong characteristics and traits. It gave me a better understanding of where Dad came from and what may have guided his life decisions.

Dad was born in 1943. His parents named him Francis P. Quinn. When he was growing up his family and friends called him Butch, and the nickname stuck. I am assuming it was to avoid confusion between him and his father, who shared the same name. His father's given name was Frank and Dad's was Francis; I am not sure why this was decided, but my dad was not a Junior. I have several pictures of Dad from when he was a youngster. Even back then he was very good looking. One particular picture of him stands out in my mind. It is a photo of him with his brother Bill and sister Maryellen when he was approximately seven years old. Dad and Bill both had on matching cowboy outfits and Dad was wearing a cowboy hat. Even at that age, I could recognize his grin and the same sparkle in his eyes.

During his younger years, Dad's main passion in life

was baseball, and he had a natural talent for the sport. Anytime people saw him, he was doing some type of trick with his baseball. He would play every chance he got. This continued through grammar school and high school. He also liked to watch games being played on television. Various family members and friends voiced many times over the years that he was the best left-handed pitcher in town. He was highlighted in different local papers where they would do little stories on him and his success on the baseball diamond.

In 1957, the National League's Brooklyn Dodgers and New York Giants played their final seasons as New York City-based franchises. This left New York without a National League team until 1962 with the creation of the Mets. I imagine that must have been something Dad was following and paying attention to, as baseball was always on his mind. However, as he was getting older, other things started to capture his attention.

Dad was a typical teenager growing up in South Buffalo. There were times when he and his friends would do mischievous teenage things, but they never actually got into any trouble with the law. He and his friend Jim would take the Number 16 bus to downtown Buffalo. They would go to the Palace Burlesque at 710 Main Street. The Burlesque was located in Shelton Square, which was sometimes referred to as Buffalo's Times Square. Dad and

Jim were able to sneak in and take in the later afternoon show on weekdays. They would be in awe of the beautiful women dancers with their veils, feathers, and fans. These women entertainers bared a lot but not all. In addition to those shows, there was also dancing, Vaudeville comedy, and short films; it was the place to go to for live music.

I would guess that Dad was not there for the music. He and Jim would buy some popcorn or candy and just take it all in. When there was a performer they really enjoyed, they would even splurge and buy a program. Dad's favorite dancer was Rose La Rose—a petite woman with dark hair, beautiful legs, and an hourglass figure. Her specialty was to perform a "reverse strip." She would appear on stage wearing very little and would then get dressed before the crowd. Again, I am only speculating, but perhaps Dad liked that she was not like all of the other dancers. She was her own person and did things her way. I also think her physical attributes may have been something that he found enticing.

Dad must have really been affected by his visits to the Burlesque when he was young. He continued to go to the "Canadian ballet" (strip club) whenever time or circumstances would allow. He liked to go with his friends or family members and would make a night of it. It was his way of bonding with the men in his circle. I imagine he was always looking to see if any of the women at the "ballet" resembled his Rose La Rose!

Dad and Jim also engaged in other activities that were typical of most young men. They both had a fondness for the drink and their drink of choice was beer, just like Frank's had been. Dad and Jim would frequent a delicatessen called Parks on the corner of South Park Avenue and Richfield Street. They were not of legal age to purchase alcohol, but when the lady who ran the store asked them if they were old enough, they simply said, "Yes we are, and we want them cold!" They would buy forty-five cent quarts of Topper beer and take them back to the roof of the Quinn's garage. They would be tipsy, but not quite drunk, after polishing off a couple of beers and they would discuss life, death, and infinity. After they were finished up on the garage roof, they would head down to the basement and play poker and three-card monte with a couple of their other buddies.

Dad had a girlfriend at the time. She was a young figure skater, and he would call her on the phone while they were all in the basement. He would lean up against the wall with the phone in one ear and his head resting on the wall. He wore so much Brylcreem in his hair that he actually left marks on the area where his head had been resting.

Although he was very good looking, he was not conceited. He always paid particular attention to his clothes and appearance. Some people even commented that he looked like Elvis Presley. He had some of Elvis's mannerisms down and he especially liked to listen to Elvis on the radio and his record player, though he wasn't much of a dancer. It was the music he loved to surround himself with.

While Dad was attending Bishop Timon High School, a private Catholic high school for boys, he had a part-time job at the Park Edge Supermarket in South Buffalo. It was there that he first set eyes on my mother Amelia (Molly), and he never took them off her after that day. She was in his heart. Dad was in love and as the Elvis Presley song goes, he was "All Shook Up."

My uncle Richard who was a teenager during Mom and Dad's courtship years, witnessed their evolving love story. They were content just to be sitting on the couch at Mom's family home. The two of them didn't need anything else other than to be together while they were dating. He said that Dad reminded him of Dean Martin and was very good looking, but he didn't look for attention. They complimented each other in terms of their looks as Mom was very pretty. However, their personalities were different from each other. Dad was more low-keyed, laid- back and even-keeled. Mom was a spitfire when provoked, very religious, and people knew where they stood with her. Her family, friends and teachers respected her. She was also somewhat fearless.

I got a better understanding of my mother's persona when my uncle shared a couple of stories about when he and Mom were young. There was a bully in the neighborhood who forced him to go down to a local park area and made him dismember worms. He was traumatized by the incident and told Mom about it. She went and found that bully and beat the crap out of him. Mom was his protector. She looked out for those she loved. Also, she was very devout in her Catholic beliefs. He remembered one time when he saw her and her friend inching their way down the street on their knees. They had their dungarees rolled up and were both just making their way up to Seneca Street. He could see that their knees were getting scraped up and he couldn't help but ask them what they were doing. Mom simply replied, "We are doing penance." Uncle Richard didn't understand what would make her feel as though she had to go to such extremes to repent for her sins since she was a young teenage girl. But then he thought, she did beat up the neighborhood bully. Maybe she did have some other skeletons in her very limited closet that required penance!

Mom and Dad dated for a couple of years and they wanted to get married, but neither of them was even 18. Therefore, Dad had to get his parents' permission to wed his Molly. They married in 1962. My mother was the light of his life and was the flame that ignited Dad. In looking at old photos of Rose La Rose, I saw a bit of a resemblance between her and Mom. Both were brunette, and of smaller stature but with ample bosoms.

Although Mom proudly celebrated Dad's Irish heritage, she was Polish and proud of it! Just as the Irish like to celebrate St. Patrick's Day by wearing green and eating corned beef and cabbage, the Polish also have celebratory festivities. Mom would participate in Dyngus Day, which is observed the day after Easter Sunday. It celebrates the end of Lent and Polish pride. Boys throw water over girls and gently spank them with pussy willows. People dance the polka and wear the colors of Poland, white and red. They eat kielbasa (sausage), pierogis, and Golabki (stuffed cabbage) and have a butter lamb on their holiday table. I like to think of it this way: Irish + Polish = our Quinn family.

THE TIMES THEY ARE A-CHANGIN'

MY PARENTS WERE settling into their married life. They had an apartment on Mineral Springs Road in South Buffalo. For a couple of years, Dad was working as a cinder dick (a nickname for railroad cop) protecting the properties, facilities, passengers, and cargo on the railroad cars. In 1965, he took the Buffalo Police Department's entrance test. He passed and was appointed to the BPD in 1966 as a temporary Patrolman, and quickly became permanent just two months later. Dad took his job very seriously and wanted to be an exemplary police officer. He looked up to his father and uncle and wanted to be like them; both being BPD Officers. They had it in their blood to protect and to serve in their community. Dad was proud to be protecting the citizens of Buffalo; he was *Buffalo Proud.*

Dad was not a violent man in any aspect of his life. He was somewhat passive. He shared an incident about a time he was on a call and encountered a man in a backyard. The man had a gun and it was pointed straight at Dad. I imagined the father I knew so well, with his calming voice and laughing eyes being able to put the man at ease. He simply said to the man, "You don't want to do this." Fortunately, the man dropped the gun and was taken into custody without incident. He had disarmed the man with only his words. In fact, most of the time he was able to perform his job without having to use physical force.

He was doing well in the department and was working on the BPD's Tactical Patrol Unit in the late 1960s. There he was assigned a partner, and they were working during the Buffalo riots in 1967. *The Spectrum*—the University of Buffalo's Newspaper—published a picture of Dad on their front page. He, along with many other police officers, had been called in to keep the peace as many students were protesting the Vietnam War. *The times they were a-changin'*, and they were very turbulent as racial tensions were at the forefront. Dad never shared his personal views about any of these riots. As a Buffalo Police Officer, he had taken an oath to protect and serve. He was doing his job, plain and simple.

There were many times I found myself wanting to ask Dad his opinion on current issues in the world. I wish I could talk to him about the situation going on now in our country with riots and protests since he lived through similar situations back in the 60s and 70s. I would also be interested to know his feelings about the anti-police sentiment that is at the forefront of the news and our own community. If only…

BPD

One incident, in particular, left an indelible mark in the hearts and minds of Dad and his partner. They were serving as back-up for a few precincts, responding to the usual calls when they were sent to West Ferry Street. Dispatch had received a call about a man with a knife who snatched a young boy that lived in the house they were responding to. Several teams of officers were all running around the neighborhood looking for the pair. They located them and the man was out of control. He grabbed the boy and ran with him to an area that had an incline. It was utter chaos for several minutes until one of the officers screamed out, "He's up here!" They ran as fast as they could, but unfortunately, they were not able to get to the boy in time. The man stabbed the boy to death. It was devastating that they couldn't save this little boy's life. They both also had to learn how to deal with the murder of a child and compartmentalize that segment of their lives that dealt with death, despair, and man's inhumanity to man. Dad and his partner had to "tuck it away" and not let it affect the rest of their lives, as they were both husbands and fathers.

Growing up, I did feel that at times Dad was overprotective of us. There were rules we had to abide by growing up that we didn't necessarily like to have to follow. We always had to tell our parents where we were going, even if it was just over to the neighbor's house. When we would walk up to the local store, we had to be back within a certain amount of time – no dilly dallying. We usually had to be in our house by dark. With there being so many kids, they had to establish some boundaries for all of us to ensure our safety. Perhaps it was incidents such as the little boy's murder that always stayed on Dad's mind. Although he had tried to "tuck it away," that may have been easier said than done.

Another time when Dad and his partner were working together, they got tangled up in a mess. On a snowy winter night, they were driving back to the police garage in separate cars. In Buffalo, the winters are brutal, with an average temperature below freezing. Although boots and gloves were part of the BPD's standard police uniform in the winter, Dad would not wear them. He would just wear his regular work shoes and no gloves.

They came upon a man in the middle of the street who refused to move. Both officers got out of their police cars and a scuffle ensued. The man grabbed Dad and was trying to punch him. His partner was hitting the man with his baton, trying to get Dad free of the man's grip. Since the ground was so slippery, Dad fell and took the man down with him. It was quite a scene as other officers arrived and found them rolling around on the ground in the middle of the street. Dad's hands were tangled in the man's hair and they became so swollen from the fist battle that later he couldn't get his wedding ring off. Fellow police officers had to take him to a place where they could cut his ring off. Fortunately, they were able to repair it and Dad got the ring back.

Back around the same time period, Dad and his partner worked as bouncers and provided security for a popular bar called "Jack's Cellar." The bar was located in the basement of the Dun Building at 110 Pearl Street on the south west corner of Pearl and Swan Street, not far from police headquarters. The building has a distinct honor of being Buffalo's first steel-framed skyscraper, and is very narrow in its architectural design. It was named for the R. G. Dun Company which later became Dun and Bradstreet, the nation's oldest and largest credit reporting agency. The patrons of the thriving bar were lawyers, newspaper reporters, office workers, and business men and women from various companies in the downtown Buffalo area. They would come to the bar after getting out of work from businesses that included Marine Midland Bank, Blue Cross/ Blue Shield, the Buffalo Evening News, the Courier-Express (local Newspaper Organizations) and numerous others in the downtown area. These professionals could come and unwind after a grueling day at the office. The bar had a cozy ambience. The lighting was kept low, and the drinks would flow. There was even a chess board that people could play while enjoying their cocktails and just relax. The men were either in suits or business casual. The women who would come were usually dressed to impress. One of my friends told me that she and her friends looked forward to going to Jack's for happy hour after getting out of work from a near-by insurance company. For the outing, she would wear fashionable dress pants or skirt, and would usually undo a button or two of her crisp, white shirt. In the 70s, it was the place to go see and be seen.

I tend to think that Dad didn't mind having this job where he was paid well to keep order in a trendy establishment that normally didn't attract a rough crowd. It was not as stressful as being out working the streets of his regular police job. He was able to be part of the scene, but from a different vantage point. For Dad and his partner, it was a great gig. They both welcomed the extra money which helped with their family financial obligations. And since this job required them to keep their eyes on all patrons, even the ones who had a few buttons undone...well, that was what they were hired to do!

Dad was persistent in everything he did on his main police job. He never gave up. He would drive up and down streets to pick out stolen cars. He was like a bloodhound; he could just sense when something was amiss. He and his father were similar in their work ethic. I imagined them both to be a "cop's cop." They didn't "polish their own badges" or "tarnish another's badge" to make themselves more favorable to the brass. They would back up their partner(s) without being asked. They were both relentless and would do whatever it took to get the job done to the best of their abilities.

In 1971, Dad transferred to Headquarters where he worked in the Narcotics Division. In less than two years he was promoted to Detective. Dad was just as ambitious as his father was with his career with the BPD and he was also just as unassuming. Dad and his former partner kept in touch over the next several years. They both had given their all to their chosen profession. They, too, were forever *bonded by the blue.*

RING OF FIRE

DAD WAS VERY busy in his professional life, and even more so in his personal life. He and Mom were blessed to have nine children in quick succession: Mary Pierre, Frank, Kim, Faith, Kenneth, Joseph, John, Christian, and Mary Gratia (Grace). I was named after a Catholic nun, Sister Mary Pierre. My sister, Mary Gratia (Grace) was named after sister Mary Pierre's sister, Sister Mary Gratia, who was also a nun. Mom had spent a great deal of time with these two nuns who lived at the Sisters of Mercy Convent on Abbott Road. She loved them both dearly and I believe she named us after them as a way of showing her respect and admiration for these two women.

These two nuns were very close to a man named Father Nelson Baker. He was a Roman Catholic priest and church administrator in the Buffalo area. When he passed away in 1936, he had already developed many structures and organizations under the patronage of Our Lady of Victory in Lackawanna, NY. His "city of charity" included a minor basilica, an infant home, a home for unwed mothers, a boys' orphanage, a hospital, nurses' home and two schools. This revered holy man is well known throughout the Western New York area and was honored as "Buffalo's most influential citizen of the 20th century. He was also dubbed the "Padre of the Poor" by the local newspapers.

Before Sister Mary Pierre passed away, she gave Mom a hand embroidered picture of the sacred heart of Jesus Christ she had made for Father Baker. Sister Pierre said that the picture hung above Father Baker's bed for many years. After Father Baker died, she was given back the picture. Mom passed that picture onto me and it is one of my most cherished possessions.

An early memory of our growing family was in 1970. I remember Mom and Dad coming back home from the hospital with one of the newborns. The older kids, myself included, loved when a new baby came into the home because our parents told us that the new baby brought along a gift for us. My particular gift with the birth of this child was a little pink and white bunny. Mom would be getting the baby's bottle ready and Dad would be sitting on the couch holding the new one. I would see him close his eyes and drop his chin and gently take in the scent of the newest baby. He loved the smell of newborn life. I don't ever recall seeing him change any of the kids' diapers or feed them, but he loved to hold them and never seemed to want to put them down. As he moved up through the ranks of the BPD and more of his children were born, those times of holding them sadly became less frequent.

Our family lived on Redway Road in Grand Island,

NY during the 70s, 80s, and 90s. We were not the typical family image. Even back in the 70s, nine children were considered a large family. Our small house had four bedrooms. One of those rooms was converted into a utility room where we would do laundry; there was also a crib for the youngest child. Doing several loads of laundry was a daily occurrence. Another room was our parents' room, and the other two were set up like military barracks. One room was for the girls and the other was for the boys. At times there were just mattresses on the floors.

We made the best of the cramped quarters and tried to keep things as tidy as possible. Everyone was assigned a couple of shelves where we each kept our clothes, as there was no room for dressers. Our house was always jam-packed with our friends and cousins who would come and stay with us at times. We really learned as a family how to make things work. We had to; there were no other options. I suppose that may be why my siblings and I turned out to be so resilient.

Sunday mornings will forever be a fond memory from my childhood. Dad did not attend mass with us. His philosophy on religion was "Dear God if there is a God, save my soul if I have a soul." He would pick us up from Mass, and rotate a few of us kids each week, so that we all had an opportunity to spend time with him and take us to the bakery across the street from the church to pick out delectable treats. We would all go back home in our trusty old beat-up station wagon and sit around the 10-foot-long kitchen table, built to fit into our small kitchen. Some of us kids would be propped up on telephone books because there was no room for highchairs. Dad would play his country music mini concert for us while we ate hard rolls, sweet rolls, and donuts. All of us kids, even the very young ones, knew the words to Johnny Cash's "Ring of Fire" before we knew the words to "God Bless America."

In addition to all the kids growing up in this small house, we had many species of mammals and reptiles roaming around. St. Francis of Assisi (patron saint of animals) was Mom's favorite Saint. She would recite the Prayer of Saint Francis to us and teach us that all of God's creatures were to be respected. There were dogs, cats, birds, hamsters, and gerbils. Then things got slippery when lizards, snakes, and iguanas were added into the mayhem. Our house was cluttered with so many of God's creatures. There was an incident where our parakeet, Peace, got out of his cage and flew right into my large dangly hoop earring. I suspect he mistook it for his perch. He got caught up in it and it tore my earlobe. I still wear that scar with a testament to my upbringing.

Dad did not like all of these creatures sharing his limited space. It was difficult enough to feed so many children, let alone all of these creatures of God on the salary of a police officer, but he just didn't know how to say no to Mom. He just loved her so much and wanted to make her happy. It wasn't that she ran the household or that what she said was the rule of the land, but since Dad was hardly ever home, someone had to take charge of our daily lives.

On occasion, as a rare treat, our family would go to Cathay Gardens, a Chinese Restaurant on Niagara Falls Boulevard. What a scene to see so many children and our parents at a giant table the restaurant workers would put together for us. I recall the workers at the restaurant were always so kind and accommodating. It was an amazing experience to order whatever we wanted. We were not accustomed to such a splurge! The attention of the other customers was also amusing to all of us. So many kids were quite the spectacle and very entertaining. We were probably good for their business. We were all well behaved and just out to dinner like any other family, but we weren't like any other family. Even then, I felt we were special. Other families in our neighborhood had a lot of kids, but my siblings and I shared a unique bond. I think we all needed that bond to get through difficult times. Of course, there were times we would fight, take each other's food and clothes, and tattletale on each other. But every night when we would go to bed, usually with other siblings in our beds, we felt lucky to have each other. We knew that our parents loved us and did the best they could to nurture us and make sure we had all of our needs taken care of.

Since there was not a lot of money for family entertainment, Dad had to think of things to do on a small budget for our large clan. Sometimes he would load all of us kids into the old station wagon and take us for a car ride. He would drive us back and forth across the Father Baker Bridge (known locally as the Skyway). The shocks on the car were so shot that when we would go over the bump, it felt like we were on a roller coaster. It was such a thrill! Dad was just happy to be spending time with us and we were so happy to be spending time with him. He was working several jobs in addition to being a police officer to keep the family secure. His time was precious and not something he could easily give us. On these memorable outings, he would play his favorite music on his 8-track player. We would listen to Marty Robbins, Merle Haggard, Willie Nelson, and Kris Kristofferson over and over again. But his all-time favorite singer was the man in black, Johnny Cash. We would all sing along to "Ring of Fire" and laugh. The entire day would cost a few dollars for gas. But for us, what we took away from those times was priceless.

Another fun thing Dad and Mom did for our family was take us all to Lake Erie State Park. The first time we went, there were only five children, so Dad rented a Winnebago. During the day we would all go on little hikes around the park. At night, he and Mom would make dinner around the campfire. After dinner, when clean-up was all done, the real fun began. We were all allowed to stay up late since we were on vacation. Dad would play his records on his portable record player. Each night, we would start with "Ring of Fire." Everyone would sing along, and he would put on another favorite—usually "El Paso" by Marty Robbins. Those of us who were old enough to speak knew most of the words and would try to remember them all so we could sing along with Mom and Dad. The little concert would go on until the last embers of the fire died. Everyone knew then that it was getting time to call it a night and go to bed when Dad would play "Ring of Fire" one last time for the evening. No one wanted to go to bed, but he would assure us that we would do the same the following evening and that pacified us.

As we outgrew the Winnebago, Dad started to rent a couple of cabins at the park. Those times were even better. They had a lot more space and all of us loved to sleep in the bunk beds that were built into the walls of the cabin. We would also bring playpens for the babies. There were no bathrooms in the cabins so we would have to use flashlights in the dark evenings to guide the way over to the restrooms that also had showers. During the days, we would all play baseball, kickball, and hide-and-seek. There were so many things to do in the spaciousness of the area where we were staying. We prepared simple meals, the best of which was Bocce pizza on the first night of the camping trip. Dad would pick up the pizzas before we set out on our venture. He loved Bocce pizza, well known in the Buffalo area for the way they packaged their pizzas for take-out in corrugated boxes. The pizza was half-baked. We would heat them up in the little oven in the cabin or just eat them cold. Even if we didn't love Bocce pizza, we never told Dad that. We were just glad to be having pizza with him.

Since there were so many things that needed to be brought on these trips, my parents would also invite other family members and their children to join us, and they would bring their own supplies and extras for anyone who needed towels, bedding, cleaning products, and food. There would be two adults and up to seven children at times staying in each of these little cabins. But no one seemed to mind the limited space.

LOVE ME TENDER

THINGS WERE AS normal as normal could be for our Quinn family. However, all of that changed when our mother went to the doctor for a persistent cough. When she and Dad came home from the doctor appointment, they sat the older kids down and talked with us about how things would be changing for our family. I was 10 years old. They explained the best way they could that our mother had lung cancer. She was going to get very sick and our family would all have to work together as a team to get through the challenging times we would be facing.

With Mom being very religious, she had faith that she would be cured of her disease. She believed in the legend of the mustard seed. It is a symbol of overcoming obstacles and she believed she would overcome cancer. I was around 11 years old when my mother decided to paint "Praise the Blessed Name of Jesus" on our garage door. She was always professing her love of God. The neighbors thought it was unusual that we had this message painted in big black letters on the garage door; people would drive by just to look at it. I too thought it was odd, but it seemed to make Mom happy for that period of time. I don't recall Dad ever saying a word about it. I believe he thought that there was no reason to say anything if it gave her comfort and strength. Many of her church friends would come and visit her to help her to keep her faith. One of them sent a picture of the painted garage door to the 700 Club with Pat Robertson. It was a flagship television program of the Christian Broadcasting Network. The show came to the Buffalo area, and the producers had our mother come on the show to interview her. It was a very moving story that she shared with the viewers. People responded to her in such a positive manner after that broadcast. It kept her spirits up and fueled her will to go on. She was a fighter. She was not only fighting for her life but the well-being of all of us. I believe she was worried about what would happen to us if she were to pass. She loved us all very much. We were her life and lifeline.

Dad was doing his best coping with our mother's disease and treatments. In the early 70s, there were medical advancements being made to combat cancer, and she was receiving good medical care. However, she was becoming much frailer with each passing month.

All of us kids felt loved by Dad, but he didn't seem to be able to say those words to us very often. He was just too busy, or maybe caught up in his life of chaos. What he couldn't say or display to us with his affections, he was able to do for our mother. The most profound gesture of love I remember Dad making was when he picked her up off of their bed, took her into the living room, and gently placed her on the couch. He knew how much she loved Cathay Gardens but she was too weak from the treatments to eat food. However, he would still continuously buy it for her. Even though she couldn't eat it, she at least was able to enjoy the smell. Dad *loved her tenderly*. He was lost in his grief of knowing that our mom, his Molly, wasn't getting any better. She was getting worse. I remember different church members coming to our home to pray with her and with us. Dad was never home for those gatherings. Looking back, I assume that it would have been too hard for him to handle. And since he was working most of the time, perhaps it was best that it worked out that way.

One of Mom's church friends offered us the use of a house she owned in Kenmore, NY. Dad moved us there for around a year. He thought it would be easier if we lived in Kenmore for our mother to get to her doctor's appointments and treatments. The house on Redway Road was put on the market. The house in Kenmore was larger with more bedrooms, so the extra space was a godsend. Mom was sick a great deal of the time so we all chipped in to do what we could. Money was very tight, but we were getting by. One thing Dad did to make Mom feel better was to organize a "special drawer" that was high up on the tallboy dresser in their room. It was out of arm's reach of most of us kids. In it, he put her special treats of Cheez-its, sour hard candies, and suckers. It was also where she kept the turbans and wigs that she wore since losing her hair from treatments. He also put bath beads and her perfume in this drawer. She found comfort in taking long baths to ease her sore, aching body, and soothe her soul.

The school-age kids in our family were enrolled in the local Catholic school. A variety of people from church would come and help out with meals and chores. They were good to Mom and to us. Grandma Eleanor (our mother's mother) also came over when she was not working. She was very close to all of us. A special bond developed between her and Dad. It was difficult enough to watch her daughter waste away from the disease, but seeing Dad do all he could do to keep us together and attempt to keep his wife content completely broke her heart.

Her world was also turned upside down when her daughter was diagnosed with cancer. She would take four buses each weekend to come and stay with us to tend to the needs of our mother and to give Dad a break. She would cook and clean for us, but more importantly, she would just talk to us. Watching our mother slip away was scary. We didn't know what to do. She would try and console us and be as positive as possible about our situation, but there were times when I would see her crying while she thought we were all playing in another room. I never went in to comfort her during those times. I thought that if I did, it would make it all too real. Although I was young, I understood that my mother was dying, but none of us ever said those words out loud.

We did not bring "An Olde Irish Toast" with us to the Kenmore house. Dad left it at the Redway Road house. That house never sold, so he moved our family back after about a year. I had reservations about returning to our old house, but it did bring feelings of comfort and familiarity into our chaotic lives. When we were living in Kenmore, life felt paused for a year. We were all together and Mom was still alive. Unfortunately, after we moved back, it seemed like things were moving in fast forward, and not in a good direction.

Now and then a few of the siblings were able to escape the turbulence of our lives for a day. Once a month, Dad would choose three kids for a special excursion to visit our Great-Grandparents, Molly and Steve (Grandmother Eleanor's parents). I thought it was for us kids, but in retrospect, I believe it was for his sanity. When we were young, we thought Irving, NY was worlds away. It's only an hour outside Buffalo, but it was a completely different universe of nurturing and love. Dad would take us there early in the morning. Upon our arrival, a magnificent breakfast of toast, eggs, and bacon would be waiting for us. I still remember the smell of the bacon. It brought me such a feeling of security and stability. It wasn't the taste of the bacon that I craved, but the memory it brought back to me. Grandma had coffee for Dad at his assigned seat. We would sit across from him and she would leave the room to tend to other things. I think she left us there to have a rare moment alone with him and share a meal in peace, as she was keenly aware that never happened back at our house.

After the scrumptious breakfast was finished, she would say, "Butch, why don't you go lay down and take a nap?" He would just look at her with such appreciation and gratitude in his eyes and say, "That would be great." For us, that was when the best things would happen. As Dad slept downstairs in the spare room, she would take us upstairs to her amazing closet that was filled with presents. We were allowed to go in and pick out items we would like. It was like Christmas, but a Christmas we never really knew. We would spend an hour up there with her after we picked out the gifts. She would show us pictures of our mother, grandmother, and all of her children. As we sat on the two twin beds in her bedroom, she would talk to us about her family and what family meant to her. Although she was not overly demonstrative with her love, as we sat across the bed from her, she would reach out and hug us. It felt like being in the arms of an angel. To me, Grandma Molly was an angel.

Another bonus to these incredible days would be when she would say, "Why don't you go into the drawers and see if there is something in there for you?" In her dresser, she would have additional gifts. These gifts were already chosen for us. She picked out clothing sets and jewelry for the girls. The boys would also have an outfit and a toy in there for them. We had never known such generosity in our lives. It wasn't so much her generosity that we appreciated; it simply was her love.

To our delight, the day was not over. She and Grandpa

Steve would drive us to the Cloverleaf Hotel. Their daughter, Madge, purchased it from them years before. When they owned it, it was called the Irving Hotel. It was on Route 5 and 20, right by New York State Thruway, exit 58, which is a cloverleaf. Having never been to a hotel before, I remember being fascinated the first time we went. I was intrigued by this long, white, two-story dwelling filled with metal tables and red chairs and a big wooden bar. Since it was still morning, it was very quiet without any patrons. However, I could hear Grandpa Steve washing the glasses behind the bar, and I could smell the lingering scent of the fried food that was served the night before. Upstairs was a functioning hotel. Madge would take us up there and we would peek into some of the empty rooms. There was a just a bed and a dresser in the rooms, but they were very clean and tidy. At the end of the hall was Madge's apartment. She, just like her mother, would give us little trinkets. Madge had a lot of costume jewelry and she would give us necklaces, earrings, and rings. She would also give us money and say, "I want you to buy yourself a little something special." The day just kept on getting better and better!

We were treated like kings or queens for the day. We were allowed to go behind the bar and get ourselves a soda from the soda gun. Aunt Madge would give us quarters to play the jukebox and we could pick any songs we wanted.

We would also play the bowling game that was in the corner. One of the greatest parts of the day would be when you went into the kitchen and she would say, "What is your heart's desire?" For me, it was always a cheeseburger and fries. She would put it on the big grill they had in the kitchen. It was done in no time and we would sit there with her, her son Bob, and Grandma Molly and have this awesome feast. I realize now that a burger and fries would not normally be considered a feast, but to me, it was one of the most unforgettable meals I ever had.

We would spend a couple of hours at the hotel and then head back to Grandma and Grandpa's. It was amazing how they could make one day so delightful for Dad and for the lucky children of the day. When we got back to their house, they would let us walk around their large backyard and the abandoned school across the back of their property line. We would peer into the windows and see desks and blackboards still in the classrooms. It was such a simple day, but it took our minds off of the complex things going on at home. By then, seven or eight hours had gone by. As we came back to the dining room, the table was set for another healing meal. Grandma would wake Dad up from his much-needed nap, and we would all have dinner together. Grandma loved to feed people. That probably came from years of working at her hotel serving thousands of meals to their many patrons.

As she would get up from the table to clear the dishes, she would reach her hand out to Dad, her great son-in-law, and slip him some money. It was their private moment, so we always pretended not to notice. A sadness began to creep in after we finished eating dinner because we knew it would soon be time to go home. Home was sad, and those unforgettable days in Irving were not.

To this day my sisters and I talk about the times we had at Grandma Molly and Grandpa Steve's. For us, it was one of our most cherished memories. We are still able to describe the exact layout of our grandparents' home. We can tell you where every table, lamp, picture, and room were located. After Grandma and Grandpa passed, we were able to take some of their dishes, pictures, and lamps for our own. I still have some of the hand-stitched pictures she made. My sisters still have some of the lamps from her bedroom and dining room with different crystal bobbles on them. Those were the only tangible items we took, but the memories our grandparents created for us with their love is what we walked away with and cherished most.

We also still talk about the remarkable gift closet and drawers with the special treasures put in there for us to find. For me, it's the smell of bacon, for my sisters, it's the smell of Dove soap that bring wonderful memories of these visits back to our minds. We were so fortunate to have our grandparents to help us through the worst of times. The Simon and Garfunkel song summarized our feelings, they were our "Bridge over Trouble Water."

By 1976, Mom was losing her battle. All the treatments she was receiving were making her very weak. The doctors decided she needed around-the-clock medical care so she was admitted to the hospital. Dad couldn't take off from work, so Mom's friends from church and some neighbors volunteered to take us kids into their homes for a few weeks. It broke Dad's heart to have to do this, but he had no other choice. Some of us were fortunate to go to good homes for that period of time. Unfortunately, a couple of us had disturbing things happen during this already tumultuous time. When all the siblings were back home together, we discussed what we had recently been through. We decided not to tell our parents of any of the negative things that happened. We didn't want them to have any more things added onto their plates that were already overflowing.

Eventually, Mom was brought home from the hospital. After we were all back together as a family, Dad realized he needed help taking care of Mom. He hired a nurse named Ann Marie. Since he couldn't be there most of the time, Ann Marie would come and stay with Mom and administer the narcotics she was taking for pain.

Dad knew Mom would not live much longer, but he

didn't want her to die in a hospital. He wanted her to take her last breath in their bed, in our home. She lingered for a couple months, giving it everything she could, until the very end when the last injection of morphine was given. Ann Marie knew that Mom's time was coming to an end and told Dad. He had each of us kids come into the room and say our goodbyes to Mom. Some of us were too young to understand what was happening. Our ages were thirteen, twelve, ten, nine, eight, six, five, two, and eleven months. We were all scattered across our front lawn, and we were crying when she was taken out the front door on a stretcher. I don't remember any of us hugging or embracing each other. We were just standing there, each lost in confusion and grief.

That was the last time we saw Mom, as it was decided it would be best if none of the kids attended her wake or funeral. Dad felt it would be too traumatic. I respected this decision that Dad made. I wasn't going to approach him and tell him that I think I should go because I wasn't upset that he didn't want all of us kids there. If I had gone, I worried that I would not be able to handle seeing Mom in her casket. She was buried in a skirt that I had helped sew for her. It gave me some peace knowing that a part of me was with her. If we were at the funeral home, church or gravesite, it would have been too difficult for Dad to try and keep all of us kids from breaking down. He needed his strength to stay focused and greet all of the many people who came to Mom's wake and funeral. It was something he just had to get through on his own. I think that he needed to put his Molly, our Mom, to rest on his terms so that he could survive and go on for all of us kids.

I remember when he came home after the first night of Mom's wake. He was dressed in a beautiful black suit, black shirt, and tie. He was sitting in his recliner chair drinking a beer. It was late at night, so I was getting ready for bed and had put white Noxzema skin cream all over my face. I sat across from him on the couch and asked him how everything went as if it was just another day. It was the first time I saw Dad cry. I didn't know what to do, so I went over to him and embraced him and sat on his lap. We cried together. When I moved back from him, I realized I got Noxzema all over his clothes and I apologized. He said, "Pierre, that is nothing you would ever have to apologize for. Clothes can be replaced, but you can't be. I love you." We both continued to cry until we started to laugh. The scene was so outlandish with my face all covered in white skin cream and Dad with it all over his chest, face and clothes. That night was my most precious moment with Dad.

Dad got through the remaining day of the wake and Mom's funeral. Mom was buried at Holy Cross Cemetery in Lackawanna, NY, the same place that his father was buried. Father Nelson Baker was also buried at Holy Cross. I felt she was in good company.

I remember all through Mom's sickness, music was always being played in our home. It seemed to lift our spirits and keep us connected. We would listen to country music and tunes that were popular in the mid-70s. My sisters and I loved the song "Rhinestone Cowboy" and my brothers loved "Kung Fu Fighting." But the music that really touched our hearts were the songs played in Dad's car on his 8-track player. He always seemed to be playing "Annie's Song" by John Denver or "Honey" by Bobby Goldsboro when we would go for rides with him to the store or run other errands. After Mom passed, my siblings and I would play both songs over and over again on our record player. There was a line from "Annie's Song," that we felt he was able to relate to because he lived it: "Let me die in your arms." We were glad for Dad that Mom did die in his arms.

In the song "Honey," a part we thought mattered most to Dad went, "And Honey, I miss you and I'm bein' good / and I'd love to be with you, if only I could." We never played those songs when Dad was home.

Another thing that reminded my siblings and me of our parents' love for each other was a replica of a piece of art in our living room. It was a statue of Rodin's "The Kiss." We don't remember if Mom bought it for Dad, or if he bought it for her. It was a symbol of their love that we all observed everyday as we passed through our living room. But after Mom passed, we didn't recall seeing the statue. Perhaps some things were too difficult to witness every day.

ROLL WITH THE CHANGES

THE YEAR 1977 was quite a turbulent time for us after Mom was gone. Despite the bedlam, Dad still got up every morning, went to his full-time job at the BPD, and his various part-time jobs. He was lost in grief and didn't know how to console his children, who were missing their Mom and the stability of a normal family life.

By no means was Dad a perfect man. He never professed to be, and we were not oblivious to his faults. However, he was our dad, and he took care of us after Mom passed to the best of his ability. Even so, Social Services came to our home to evaluate our situation. I am not sure how they were notified. Perhaps my poor attendance record at school was a contributing factor? I missed many days of school to stay home and take care of my siblings when they were sick. Social Services considered it too much for a single man to be able to look after all of us, especially since we were all under the age of 14. They wanted to put all of us into foster homes. There was no way he was going to let that happen! Dad was able to hire a local woman from Grand Island to come in and assist with babysitting, cooking, and cleaning during the week. It gave him peace of mind to know we were being looked after, and

Social Services stopped coming to our house.

Dad worked extra part-time jobs to afford to pay the woman who was looking after us and to keep a roof over our heads, although the roof was badly in need of repair. He kept food on our table. Starkist Tuna was a staple in our little house, along with Kraft macaroni and cheese. To this day, I still have conflicting emotions every time I eat a tuna sandwich. Dad also seemed to hug us more often. We all needed that.

We were also fortunate to have Grandma Eleanor come and spend weekends with us when she didn't have to work. She and Dad became even closer during that time. She treated him as if he were her own son. He was also good to her in his own way. She loved perfume and he would always make sure she had her favorite, "White Shoulders." I remember seeing them sometimes sitting at the table, her with her tea and him with a Budweiser. She would make him lunch and although there were not many words spoken, you could feel their bond. We wouldn't go into the room during those private moments, as we realized they both desperately needed that time together. She wanted to console him for what he was going through losing his wife, and he wanted to do the same for her, having lost her daughter.

In the midst of all the pandemonium, Dad was still able to look out for me. It was around the time he had become a detective; I was very proud of him when I learned this. My class was given an assignment of "Show and Tell." We all had to bring in an item from home and explain to our class why we chose that particular item. I had no idea what to bring and I must have discussed my dilemma with my family. The very next day, Dad came to me with a free-standing poster board that had pictures laminated onto it which identified different categories of drugs. He spent some time explaining things to me that were on the board. I took notes and then worked on putting together my brief presentation for a couple of days. I was nervous to have to get up in front of my classmates and do the presentation, but also a bit excited to go to school the next day; that was a rarity.

I was nervous while listening to some of the other classmates who went before me. One had brought in her two gerbils in a little cage and the other brought in his fishing pole and tackle box. I got up there and popped open my posterboard and did my presentation with staunch resolve. I realized that I did a good job when I heard my classmates' enthusiastic chatter and the reoccurring comment was "That's cool!" I was the girl of the hour (closer to 5 minutes). Up until that point, I didn't think Dad was even aware of all that was going on in our muddled lives. There were just so many kids, grocery shopping trips, doctor appointments, school meetings, etc. But by his gesture of taking the time to help me out with my "Show and Tell" assignment, he showed me that he was listening, and he had our backs. And I was able to tell my class how proud I was of Dad for being a Buffalo Police Detective.

In return, I always tried to help out Dad as much as I could, but I was only 13. Several neighbors and church members generously donated food for our first Thanksgiving following Mom's passing. Since Dad and Grandma Eleanor both had to work that day, and our babysitter was with her own family, cooking our dinner was left to me. I remember I would watch Graham Kerr from the Galloping Gourmet show on TV, and I thought that preparing our meal would be a cinch since he was able to put a gourmet meal together in one hour or less. But since I was so young and inexperienced with cooking, I was unaware of the ratio of pounds to hours required to cook poultry and I massively miscalculated. Apparently, one hour is not enough cooking time for a 16-pound turkey! Fortunately, Dad was not home to witness or be part of the undercooked turkey debacle. Within hours of the "feast" I prepared, we were all running to the bathrooms in our house. Since there were only two, the bushes out front provided a makeshift bathroom for those not fortunate enough to get a coveted seat inside.

To this day, I have never prepared another turkey or Thanksgiving dinner for my family. It is always at another family member's home; usually one of my sisters will host. My siblings assure me it is because my home is too small to accommodate all of us. I believe they are just being polite and don't want to hurt my feelings. But more realistically, I believe they don't want to relive the food poisoning incident of 1977. Some things are just way too painful.

Months later it was still obvious that Dad's heart was completely broken, but he knew he needed to persevere for us. He continued his career with the BPD and was making a good income. However, there were outstanding costs from our mother's medical care. Coupled with his kids getting older, the expenses continued to increase. He kept working part-time jobs at Jenss Department Store and various construction sites as a security guard. While working at Jenss, he met a young woman named Michele who worked security for a different store in the same mall. Both being part Irish, there was a little spark when they met. They both wisely thought it best to be just friends. Michele went on to work at the BPD as a civilian employee and later in community engagement work.

Dad was missing something in his life. He was lonely and he craved normal family dynamics. After several months went by, we noticed he was going out more in the evenings. When he found some time to himself, he liked to go to bars for live music entertainment. He was always very particular about his appearance and grooming. However, he seemed to be wearing more fashionable clothes, and I remembered he smelled really nice. Eventually, we figured out why he seemed to be happier than he had been in a long time. It was at the Bonnet Bar in Tonawanda, NY that he met a young woman named Mary.

I was happy for him to find love again in his life. He needed that, and he needed to bring some normalcy back into our lives. However, I also experienced some resentment with there being a new woman taking center stage in Dad's life. For the period of time since Mom's passing, I was the woman of the house. I felt that my position was being threatened.

When Dad had all of us meet Mary for the first time, I remember thinking that she looked like Farrah Fawcett who was on a TV show called "Charlie's Angels." Her hair looked just like Farrah's and I liked the outfit she had on. It was a pair of jeans with a red hooded sweater that had a blue stripe along the sleeves and a pair of fashion boots. I remember thinking I wish I had clothes like that. It was a difficult first meeting for me as I was still so sad and missing Mom. Also, with Mary being only 14 years older than me, I did feel some competition for Dad's attention and affection.

After Dad had been dating Mary for several months, she moved into our home. She did bring some much-needed law and order into our lives. It was a total adjustment period for all. I vaguely recall that during that time period, some of Mary's pretty shirts may have gone missing. Dad chalked it up to my rebellious teenage years. I went with that.

Within the year, Dad and Mary were married. It was 1978 when they had a Catholic Church wedding at St. Stephen's Church on Grand Island on a hot summer day in August. Both of Mary's parents walked her down the aisle of the church. Mary's dress was a beautiful, white, simple gown, and she wore a fashionable white hat. Mary had two of her girlfriends stand up with her and Dad also had two of his friends with him at the altar. One of them was his former partner and good friend, Ronny Coyle.

Since I didn't have a nice dress to wear to their wedding, Mary generously let me borrow a pretty black dress of hers. It was a simple, off the shoulder outfit with a cinched waist. I remember all of my other siblings also found nice clothes to wear that day. Some of them were so young that I don't think they quite understood what a wedding was. However, some of them did come to understand that they now had a new mom.

After the ceremony, we all headed over to the Bedell's Candlelight Restaurant and Lounge on Niagara Street in Tonawanda for the reception. It was a very nice event with many children running around having a good time. I was allowed to bring my friend Patty with me. We would sneak drinks when we thought no one was looking. Again, those darn rebellious teenage years!

All of us kids were taken home before the end of the reception. Understandably, our parents wanted to continue to celebrate their wedding without having to worry about all of us. Dad and Mary went away for a couple of days to Toronto for their honeymoon. They couldn't pick up and leave all of us to go away for longer than a weekend as they had many family obligations and responsibilities.

There were nine children who needed a mother, and Mary took on this very large responsibility. Not many women would marry a man with that many children, but she loved Dad and he loved her. From that point on, we were a family. I made a conscience decision to try and make this new family arrangement work. I did that for Dad. Thinking over all that he had gone through with our Mom's sickness and passing, I realized this man deserved a break in his life. We were all starting a new chapter in our family's life and I did not want to be the one to rock the boat. I would do my best to make things go as smooth as possible as we transitioned into this new venture.

With our stepmother also having the same first name as my sister and me, it did add to some confusion in our home. We now had a third Mary to join our ranks. Mary was working and contributing to the insurmountable expenses associated with a family of 11. I thought of ourselves as the Brady Bunch and then some. Our family was blessed when our youngest sister, Kelly, was born. Since I was the oldest and she was the youngest, I thought of her as my bookend.

We were all settling into our new home life with Mary and *rolling with the changes.* Of course, there were fights and differences of opinions, but we were able to come together as a family. Since Dad was busy working, he was not at home very often. However, when he was able to enjoy a night off, he would spend it with all of us. Mary worked at the Royal Pheasant Restaurant on Forest Avenue, so they would take us there for special occasions. The management and staff were great to us. The most fantastic times there were when we would go for our Christmas dinner. We would be given their special room in the back. It eventually became the one time a year we would all go out to dinner as a family.

It was a really nice change of pace for us. We were all allowed to order whatever we wanted and most of us did! There were lobster shells and butter everywhere. They gave us plastic lobster bibs to wear. We loved those bibs and would take them home with us and wear them for a couple of days. It was just so incredible to be there with Dad, who seemed to be so happy for that period of time.

He would have a couple of his Southern Comforts and actually seemed to relax. He didn't do that often. To this day, lobster is my favorite food. I am not sure if it is the taste or the memory of eating it with him.

It wasn't until recently that I found out my brother John always ordered the least expensive dinner item on the menu. It was the Virginia Baked Ham. He told Dad that it was his favorite but that was not true. He knew Dad didn't have much money and he felt bad ordering an expensive item. Dad always made us his first priority, and it touched me to know that my brother also had Dad's back in some small way.

LEAN ON ME

THE YEARS PASSED and our lives were moving forward. After Dad remarried, we did not see Grandma Eleanor as often. However, he would sometimes take us to her house so we could spend time with her. In 1981 when I graduated from high school, I moved in with her while I attended Trocaire College. I was sad to be leaving Dad and my siblings behind, but I knew I had to make a change in my life if I was going to make something of myself. All the years of dealing with my Mom's sickness and death and taking care of all my siblings left me a bit tattered. It was odd for me to think about only myself. I was entering a good point in my life.

It was while I was living with Grandma Eleanor that I learned about her hard life. She was a very proud Polish woman living in South Buffalo, married to our grandfather who was a Probation Officer. They had a good life, but it all came crashing down when he could no longer work due to severe alcoholism. Eventually, she had to divorce him. She still had her youngest son at home and had to find work. She was not above doing whatever it took to make sure they had food and kept their home. She started off as a cleaning lady at the old Meyer Memorial Hospital. Management saw her attention to detail and her dedication to the job. She took four buses a day to get to and from work. She moved up to Supervisory Housekeeper, and she wore her name badge with that title with such pride. For many years, she also had a part-time job cleaning a dentist's office. Grandma Eleanor was tireless.

It was because of her generosity in offering me a place to live and paying for part of my textbooks that I earned my degree. Every morning we would have tea together and talk in her small kitchen around her heating vent. She would sometimes sit in her rocking chair and let me rub her aching hands and back. We would discuss politics, religion, and (most surprisingly to me) sex. Grandma was an avid reader and very knowledgeable, although she never had any formal education. I believe that is why she wanted me to get my degree. She wanted me to have a better life than the one she had, and she thought education would do that.

After I graduated from Trocaire College, I moved into the dorms and attended Buffalo State College. Although she wasn't financially able to help me with my tuition, she always found a way to give me money for my books.

Grandma said her proudest day was when I graduated from Buffalo State and I wore her prized black dress with a piped white lapel. She was a chic, impeccable dresser. She would always wear her beautiful high-heeled shoes, and have her hair and make-up done, even to go to the B-Quik store up on Seneca Street. She taught me that people are judged on how they present themselves to others. She continued to work for the next several years, and she also took in my two other sisters when they graduated from high school. They both earned their degrees—Kim in Nursing and Faith in Human Services. I believe it was my grandmother's caring demeanor that guided their career choices. We could always *lean on her.*

Grandma's favorite thing to do in her spare time was garden. She would come to my house and plant my flowers for me. When she had to move into an apartment and then into a nursing home, my sisters and I took her plants out of her house and even transplanted some of her prized blooming flower bushes into our backyards. Some of those bushes are still blooming to this day, and oddly, her white roses bloom into November. We take that as a sign she is always with us. To us, she was our substitute mother. She was filling that role for her daughter who could no longer be there for us.

HERO

All of my siblings and I continued on with our lives as we transitioned from childhood into adulthood. I started my Federal career with the VA Regional Office and then the U.S. Army Corps of Engineers. Things were going well, but I was missing something in my life - I wanted to share my life with someone.

In October of 2005 I was fortunate that I had found my special person and was marrying him. I was in my early 40's and the time was finally right. I married my friend, Gene, who I first met and casually dated for over 10 years, before deciding he was the one. When I first met him, he had young children, and I wasn't prepared to make that part of my life. I was only 10 years into my Federal job and wanted to make that my main priority. I dated other people regularly over the next several years. However, I just did not find the right person for me. All the while, Gene and I would see each other at work functions I would have, and we truly were friends. I felt I could tell him anything and he was always there. After I stopped seeing a person that he knew of, I saw Gene at one of my Happy Hour events and just looked over at him in a different way. He had always been asking me out on more dates, but I didn't see the point until that one evening.

The following Monday when we were both at work in the Federal Building in downtown Buffalo, I went to his office and asked him if he would take me out to dinner. He gladly accepted my proposal and we went to Niagara Falls, Canada that weekend for dinner at Casa D'Oro, one of Dad's favorite restaurants. After that weekend, we started dating regularly. It was a couple of weeks later that I took Gene to meet my family. I especially wanted for Dad to meet him. After that initial meeting, Gene became a regular at our family gatherings. He fit right in. Dad accepted him even though he didn't much care for Budweiser or Southern Comfort. Gene was, and still is, a bourbon and scotch drinker. I think Dad was just happy for me that I finally met someone that I was willing to bring into the family fold. Dad also was pleased that Gene knew how to play pinochle, one of his favorite card games. Gene was in!

We dated for a couple of years and talked about marriage. At that point, I was ready and willing, but he had a great deal going on his life. His youngest son was murdered and the turmoil that went along with that horrific time in his life, left him depleted. I patiently waited for him to get to a place in his life where he could see us being married, all the while hoping that we someday would. I even went to a jewelry store and picked out a ring that I would like if he were ever to engage me. I gave him a picture of the ring and where he could purchase it. Around a year went by but no ring. I had pretty much given up on our getting engaged. Gene and I both liked to travel and we went on a Caribbean Cruise that left out of New Orleans. Much to my surprise, while we were on a little boat going down the Rio Grande River in Jamaica, a little box appeared in Gene's hand. When he opened it, there was the exact ring I had given him a picture of. The only difference was that he supersized the diamond!

From that point on, I was like every other middle-aged woman, excitedly planning our wedding. I wanted it to be just the way we wanted it, and it was! Since we would not be having an actual Church service, we decided to have the wedding ceremony at what was previously the Holiday Inn on Grand Island. The officiant for the ceremony was Robert (Bob) Fink. I had served on the Buffalo Police Commissioner's Citizen Advisory Group (CAG) with him for many years. In addition to his position of Chairperson of the CAG, he was also a Chaplain with Hospice. Many of my friends and my sister Faith knew Bob through Hospice. Gene and I felt he would be the perfect person to marry us.

We wanted our wedding to be in the fall and I thought

that having it on my brother John's birthday would be perfect. So, on that cool, crisp, beautiful autumn afternoon in October, Gene and I said "I do" in front of all of our family and friends. I wore a simple white gown with my hair in an updo with a small tierra. Gene was dapper in his black tuxedo. Our wedding colors were black, white, and accents of red.

Dad walked me down the aisle to give me away. He looked so handsome in his black suit and he was wearing a vibrant colored tie with our wedding colors. I remember turning my head and saying to him, "Great tie." He always made a point of having a perfectly matched tie for the occasion.

My friend Carmela was my maid of honor, and Gene's son, Jeff, was his best man. There were red roses in the room where we had the ceremony and even more of them in the room where the reception took place. We had scratch-off tickets on the tables for every one of our guests. By having the ceremony and the reception all in the same basic location, it made logistics easier. We also had it at a hotel, so that people could get a hotel room for the night and not worry about drinking and driving. Of course, there was an open bar for the entire affair. We insisted on top shelf so that Dad's Southern Comforts could be available to him.

Our wedding was not the traditional Buffalo, NY wedding. We wanted it to be more of a party than a wedding. When people walked into the beautiful room with a large bar and cocktail tables placed throughout that reception area, they were surprised that the music was already in full throttle. It wasn't blaring, but we all started dancing right at the beginning. I was a dance instructor for many years and all of my "girls" were there with me to celebrate this day.

After the first hour of cocktails, we invited our guests to partake in the five different food stations we had set up along the perimeter of the large room. People commented that they loved the entire flow of the reception. They could eat, drink and dance at their leisure. There was not a formal structure to the event; it was an amazing party from start to finish.

Gene and I did have our first dance together around an hour into the festivities. We chose the song, "God Bless the Broken Road" by Rascal Flatts. After we finished, I then had Dad come to the dance floor for our Father Daughter Dance. Dad was not a very sentimental person, but I felt an overwhelming connection to him when he and I danced to the song I had chosen which was Mariah Carey's, "Hero." I put a great deal of thought into which song would the best one for him and I to dance to. I always found it difficult to communicate to Dad just how much I loved him, and that I somewhat understood all that he went through with Mom's passing. By choosing that song, I didn't have to physically say the words. Instead, I let Mariah do it for me—And then a hero comes along with the strength to carry on, and you cast your fears aside and you know you can survive. / When you feel like hope is gone, look inside you and be strong. / And you'll finally see the truth, that a hero lies in you.

I kept it together for most of the song without crying too much. But at the end, I gave him a kiss on his cheek and said, "To me Dad, you will always be my hero." I had to go and compose myself after the dance. However, I again became very emotional when I did the following dance with my Grandmother Eleanor. It was our "Grandmother-Granddaughter Dance." I chose the song "Wind Beneath My Wings," by Bette Midler. Eleanor was the wind beneath my wings and her love and support always kept me afloat.

Everyone who attended had a great time and seemed sad to know the party was coming to end. Gene, I, and our family and friends didn't want to leave when the party was over, so at least half of the people still present, went to the bar inside the Holiday Inn. We all stayed there until last call. An absolutely good time was had by all!

A week after our wedding we went on another Caribbean cruise for our honeymoon. This time we left out of Puerto Rico. We had a great time there, but we were ready and excited to get back home and start our new life together. Just like many marriages, it hasn't always been smooth sailing for Gene and me. However, we are committed to our marriage and recently celebrated our 15-year anniversary.

I was so glad that Gene and I were able to share this very special day with Dad. Every time I hear the song "Hero" on the radio, I think back to our dance and all the emotions come running back. I know I am blessed to have him as my hero.

INTO THE MYSTIC

Several of us siblings were now married, and some were raising families of their own. However, Dad was a constant in our lives. We made it a point to see him as much as possible, especially on Father's Day, Easter, Christmas, New Year's, Halloween, and his birthday. Those who could not physically be with him would call. We also had family get-togethers when time allowed, with those of us who lived locally. We needed that bond with him.

Since many of my siblings lived out of town, we decided to have full family reunions every two years. The first few started in North Carolina in the early 2000s. After moving the reunion to different locations, we settled back in North Carolina. Between all the siblings, their spouses or significant others, our parents, and all of the grandchildren who were able to make it, we would rent a house large enough to accommodate 30 to 40 people! We would have good food, plenty of drinks, great music, and each other's company. There was laughter, tears, and disagreements. I remember at one of the reunions, my sister Kim would play a little snippet of a song on her phone or cd player and everyone would have to guess what the song was. We also would make song requests. One requested song was

Van Morrison's "Into the Mystic." Several of us were crying because we felt the song made our hearts swell with both happiness and sadness. We realized we were blessed to have each other and be together. However, we also realized that life is short and perhaps at the next reunion, we may be missing some of us. I will always remember that night, with all of us together, going *into the mystic.*

Perhaps the most profound reunion we had was in Naples, New York. Gene has a small vineyard there and he had an 850 square foot deck built onto his little Berry-Picker house which allowed us to be together in one place for meals and socializing. Since the main house was not large enough to accommodate 40-plus people, several siblings brought tents. It was an astounding sight to see ten different colored tents lined up against the backdrop of the beautiful vineyard. We rented portable toilets and had one shower available to all. For entertainment, we had what we called "The Running of the Grapes." Everyone would pour a drink of their choice and have to run from the top of the hill down to the little pond and back. Whoever had the most of their drink left in the cup won a small prize. Even the children participated with grape juice in their cups. We also had bonfires at night and would sing our family songs.

Dad had a wonderful time at that reunion. He was our "king" and we treated him like one. He never had to move far from his seat on the deck. He even participated in our hayrides without the hay. Everyone got into the trailer attached to Gene's tractor. He would take everyone through the vineyard down to a special oak tree at the end of the property said to be over 350 years old. The tree stands over 60 feet tall and has a trunk approximately seven feet wide. People have said this tree and the area it is on was where the Native American Indians would gather for pow-wows. We all got out of the trailer and formed a circle around the tree holding hands. It was a sight to be seen.

However, the most memorable time we had during that reunion was one starlit night when all 40 of us laid down on the ground and formed a hand-holding chain. We had the song "Into the Mystic" playing. There is strength in numbers, and I felt our strength that night. It was magical.

THESE ARE DAYS

IN 2011, MY siblings and I were working on having a book published. It was entitled, *The Bind that Ties.* To be able to have a way for all of us to be together and collectively work on the book, we rented a home in West Virginia for a weekend. We all met there. Some of us were coming from New York, others from North Carolina and one from New Mexico. Those who were coming from New York brought Dad. We didn't want to disrupt our working weekend by having to go out to meals, so we all brought groceries, some prepared meals, wine, beer, and Southern Comfort for Dad.

We let Dad know he did not have to contribute to the book at all if he was not comfortable. But we all secretly hoped he would open up to us and share his heartfelt feelings about his time with the BPD, our family, and our deceased mother.

To work on the introduction for the book, each sibling was asked to leave the room one at a time. This was done so the other siblings could write an opening introduction based on the collective thoughts about the missing sibling. It was difficult to have ourselves exposed and open in this way. Some of the things that came out were raw and painful to hear. However, before we started the process, we all promised each other that no one could walk away from our weekend with negative feelings toward each other.

The weekend was tumultuous, heated, loving, and healing. One of the things that came out of the many conversations we had was that not all of us agreed with the decisions Dad made regarding the aftermath of Mom's death. Dad shared with us why he did the things the way he did. He made his decisions based on our family as a whole and what he thought was best for the entire group. However, some siblings felt they should have been allowed to go to Mom's wake and funeral. They felt by not being there, they did not have proper closure of her death. We realized we couldn't go back in time and do things over, but it was good that we were able to have this open communication with Dad. We never really had the opportunity to do that before. For those two nights, we gathered around the campfire and sang our songs. The ring of fire never burned so bright or mattered as much as it did those two evenings. It was difficult for adults with family obligations to come from different parts of the country for only a weekend. But we all made it happen. We did it for our family and we did it for ourselves. Perhaps someday we will get *The Bind that Ties* published. It would be another way to honor Dad and have a piece of our family's history put on paper. As the weekend progressed, we all thought, "These Are Days" by the 10,000 Maniacs was what we were living. We took a group photo on the second day we were there. The time we shared with Dad will be remembered as one of the most unforgettable experiences of our lives. Not only did I learn more than I ever had before about my family and Dad that weekend, but I also learned a great deal about myself. My take away from this experience was that I was so honored to be a Quinn and to be Dad's daughter.

LACE AROUND THE MOON

MILESTONE BIRTHDAYS FOR both my father and I occurred in 2013. I was turning 50 and Dad was turning 70. My family told me we would be having a surprise party for Dad at the Holiday Inn on Grand Island. We all went to work finding photos of him, our family, and his friends for this party. Invitations were sent, and those of us throwing the party planned the decorations and other special touches.

To my surprise and delight, all my siblings who lived out of town arrived the night before. I thought it was wonderful that they wanted to be there for Dad on this special birthday and hoped he would be surprised when he entered the room. The real surprise was when I walked into the room with him and stepped to the side so everyone could yell "Happy Birthday" to him. They were also saying happy birthday to me. It was a co-birthday celebration for Dad and me.

I couldn't believe it. I was dumbfounded, honored, and beside myself with happiness. What a family I have that they would do this for both of us. I still believe Dad thought the party was for me, and I thought it was for him. There was a D.J., an open bar and a scrumptious buffet.

Gene knows how much I love potatoes, so he made sure a mashed potato bar was part of the surprise. The room was decorated in hot pink for me and black for Dad. There were decorative shoes and mustaches all over. I love shoes and Dad had always been known for his mustache.

We had the time of our lives. After I returned home that night, I took one of the mustache stickers from the party and put it on the inside of the closet door in my bathroom. I don't have "An Olde Irish Toast" plaque on the back of my bathroom door. But every morning when I wake up and open the door and see that mustache sticker, I say, "Morning, Dad!"

That evening was one of the best times I ever had with Dad. We didn't even spend much time together since we both had friends and family members from out of town to catch up with. We would periodically catch each other's eyes and just smile. That is all we needed. I am not sure what was going through his mind. But before that night, I had not thought of how, for a short period of time, I was his one and only daddy's girl. I hoped that when he looked at me that night, he was proud of his little girl who had grown into a woman.

While the joint birthday party was more than I could have dreamed of, it was what happened the night before that profoundly changed my life. My family members who lived locally met up with the out-of-town siblings for a dinner at my sister's house. I was so happy we were all together and spending time with Dad. When I returned home that evening, I sat in my backyard just thinking of the night's events. I was also getting excited about the party the next day. As I looked up, the way the moonlight was illuminating the nearby leaves, it made it look as if there was lace around the moon. I got a pad of paper and a pen and wrote the poem "Lace Around the Moon." I wrote it for Dad. The following are a couple of sentences from the song inspired by my poem: It all depends on how you look at it, and what your mind's eye can see. / All I ask is that you'll think of me. / Whenever you look up and see the lace around the moon, know that our hearts will be together soon. / With this we will never be apart.[9]

I believe the words can speak to all of our hearts as we all have someone in our lives that we have loved and for whatever reason, we are not with them. I had my poem turned into a professionally recorded song using two local singers and musicians. I also had it copyrighted. "Lace Around the Moon" is the title of the second book I had published. Unfortunately, my father passed away before I was ever able to share the song with him. But every time I look up and see the lace around the moon, I feel he is there.

LIVING IN A MOMENT

One of Dad's favorite holidays was St. Patrick's Day. To celebrate, we would sometimes go to the parade in downtown Buffalo on Delaware Avenue. Buffalo's parade is one of the largest in the country, with tens of thousands of people attending, even when the weather does not cooperate. Since it takes place in March, there is sometimes snow on the ground and the average temperature is around 40 degrees. My workplace social group would hold a St. Patty's day luncheon every year, and we could bring our family to the party. My group was always the largest one there. It was wonderful to be able to view the parade from the second floor of the building and see a sea of green stretching down for blocks. It was also a bonus to be indoors and have the bathrooms readily available.

Dad joined us there for a few of these luncheons, and he had a great time. The best part of the day was when we would all get together for our corned beef and cabbage dinner. Mary would always have dinner ready for us after we returned from the day's activities. We would all gather in our parents' finished basement with a beautiful bar on which Dad hung all types of Irish sayings, nostalgic signs, and his collection of bobble-heads proudly displayed all around. When we sat down for our feast, he rarely ate the corned beef or potatoes, and especially not the carrots. He was never partial to vegetables. The food never mattered to him. He just cared about all of us being together, *living in our moment*. He surprised us when he started wearing a plastic Irish vest to our St. Patty's Day dinners. He was somewhat conservative in the way he dressed, so we all got a kick out of it when he would put the silly vest on and even let us take a picture.

Several of my nieces took Irish dance lessons, and would sometimes perform at different venues, including the Niagara Falls Convention Center for the holiday. We would bring snacks and combine a few tables to accommodate our large group. Inspired by my nieces' beautiful dancing, I started to take Irish dance lessons at the Irish Center on Abbott Road. Once I learned a few of the simple dances, we would all dance together at our house parties. Our times together were simple ones. But to us, they were the best of times. Simply having Irish music playing, food on the table, drinks in our hands, and Dad smiling; we were in Irish heaven on earth.

As a family, we started to do the Buffalo Pedal Tour in 2014. It is a way to see Buffalo (the Queen City) on a pedal-powered pub-crawler. It is a bike that holds up to 15 people. We always went on the Canalside Bar and Pub Crawl which visited some of the bars, breweries, and restaurants in the heart of downtown Buffalo's waterfront revitalization. Since there were so many of us, we had to reserve two bikes to accommodate all 30 of us, the food, and libations we would bring along. On our maiden voyage, we didn't know what to expect. Our sister Mary Grace made a playlist of songs we had given her earlier in the week. When the music began to play, we were transported to a different world. Enthusiastically, we set off to get some physical activity; pedaling to make the bikes move. We would pedal to the first bar stop, get off, and go into the establishment for some drinks. Bar owners and patrons would be in awe of the large clan converging on their establishment. Drinks were flowing, and we were dancing and having a grand old time. Dad would usually sit outside, never with his back to the door, and just take it all in. It was interesting to see how people would respond to him in these situations. Everyone would want to talk to us and ask questions about our family. We always loved to introduce these spectators to Dad. He had an indescribable charisma that drew people to him. He was always gracious and polite to them when they would marvel at the large family he had. I could see it in his smiling blue eyes that he was proud when people would tell him how lucky he was to have such a close-knit, beautiful family.

On our second year of the bike tour, we went to dinner at a restaurant in the Canalside area before we loaded ourselves onto the bikes. All of us who were on these outings believe it was Dad who had the best time. He would usually sit at the head of the bike where he did not have to pedal. He would sip a Budweiser and look around at all of us. He didn't say much, but he didn't have to. We could see in his eyes that he was in his element; he was with his family and we were all basking in his presence. We eventually realized it was more fun to stay on the bike singing, eating, and drinking than to go into the bars. The last tour we went on with Dad was his favorite. At the end of the night, he said, "I had the best f***ing time of my life!" When the tour was over, we would go to the Buffalo Riverworks Restaurant for a nightcap before heading back home. We were disappointed when we realized the night would be coming to an end, but we always promised we would do it again the following year. Unfortunately, that did not happen.

"I had the best f***ing time of my life!"

OH! MY PAPA

DAD WAS SO proud to see all his kids grow up, move out of the family home, and some go on to college. He was even happier to see some marry and eventually have children. His 19 grandchildren and 4 great-grandchildren were the most wonderful thing to him. Most called him Pa-pa. The ones who lived locally would come and have sleepovers at our parents' house. He doted on them during those memorable times. I think he was able to give them his love and affection so much more easily than he had with us kids because at that point in his life he had so much more spare time. He retired from the BPD in 1997 and was only working one part-time security job at the Seneca Niagara Casino.

Dad and Mary were able to travel and enjoy their lives together, but what they loved to do more than anything was to have the family to their home for get-togethers. They had a beautiful backyard with an inground pool. Dad loved his pool and he particularly loved sharing it with his grandchildren. Every summer weekend, we would all be together around the pool sharing food, songs, and drinks with each other.

There was one thing I always found so endearing when I would go over to visit with my parents. I would pull into their driveway and see Dad at the wheel of his car with one of his grandchildren on his lap. The car was not running, and the kid was doing the "steering!" They would always be laughing when I would walk past them into the house. I didn't want to disturb their special moments together. They loved spending time with Dad without having to be doing much of anything. Dad's grandchildren loved him in return. I could see it in their eyes when they looked at him and would stand in front of him to demand, "Up!" He would bend down, pick them up, embrace them for a slight moment, and then lift them up the sky. *Oh, they loved their Pa-pa.* To them, he was so wonderful. Dad knew he was blessed to have these amazing grandchildren. I saw it in his eyes every time he would pick one of them up, lay one of them down, or simply spend time surrounded by the masterpieces he played a role in creating.

SUNDAY MORNIN' COMIN' DOWN

FOR THE NEXT couple of years, things were going well for our family. However, that all changed in August of 2015 when Dad was diagnosed with lung cancer. He told us he was going to fight it—and fight it he did. He went for chemo and radiation starting in October. But he took a turn for the worse from the chemo around the holidays. He was in and out of the hospital. My sisters, Mary, and I would take turns spending nights with him at the hospital. He didn't talk much during those evenings. But that didn't matter; we were there with him, one on one. We would watch TV and help him to get in and out of the restroom. The doctors eventually let him go back home. My sister Kim would come over to the house and give him liquid supplements through his feeding tube. She would also give him his insulin shots, as his sugar levels were dangerously high. Mary also learned how to take care of some of his medical needs, and Hospice nurses would come to the house as he continued to slip away. While he was still conscious, he was struggling with metaphysical issues. He asked for our brother Kenny, who is very spiritual, to come and see him. Unfortunately, that was not possible as he was out of the country. Instead, the Buffalo Police

Chaplain came to see Dad to try and help him with his concerns. We were also fortunate that Mary's cousin is a priest, and he came to speak and pray with Dad.

Before he was no longer able to coherently communicate, Dad had a conversation with former Erie County Sheriff Thomas Higgins. I was surprised when I went to visit Dad and saw the Sheriff sitting in the chair in Dad's living room. I introduced myself to him as Dad's oldest child. Higgins said, "I just stopped by to see how my friend is doing." I hadn't even known the two of them were friends. I didn't want to intrude on their conversation, so I sat there taking it all in while the two of them talked about "the good old days," as if nothing was amiss.

I couldn't believe how Dad's entire demeanor changed when he was talking with the Sheriff. For a brief time, he had a sparkle in his eyes. He was back to being the proud police officer. He wasn't the sickly man, in a chair, in pajamas with tubes coming out of him. Dad was in his element. Talking about his time "on the job" brought him back to life, but only for a short time. That was when I realized how much he really did love his job as a police officer. It made him whole. I also realized how truly *bonded* the men and women who wear the blue are. Even though both of these men had long since retired, their *bond of blue* had not diminished.

That weekend Dad was moved from his house and

taken to Hospice. Dad passed that Sunday morning. He fought for his life until the very end, just as his Molly had. The night before, we all gathered for what actually did turn out to be our "Last Supper." Dad wasn't sitting in the kitchen with us. He was down the hall in a separate room.

The people at Hospice were amazing. They let us bring in a complete dinner, and we set the table with an Irish theme in Dad's honor. We even had a little bar set up off of the room (of course we did). We all sat at the table trying to act as if it were just another weekend of us getting together to play cards or board games. But those things did not happen. My brothers Frank, Joe, John, and Christian were there from out of town. Our other brother, Kenny, was not able to make it back. Even Dad's sister Maryellen and her husband Gene had made it in from out of state.

That night, my brothers had to leave to go back home to North Carolina. A few people stayed on, including my sister Faith. She was in the room with Dad when she saw that he was having delirium and it and it worried her. She went out to the sunroom of the hospitality suite just to clear her head, but that did not happen. She experienced "a rush of energy" which she felt was coming from our brother Kenny, who still was not able to get back home. She took it as a sign.

I originally told my sisters I wouldn't be coming that morning, but I would try to make it in the evening. However, something told me to go back there that morning. When I arrived, my heart was torn between happiness and sadness to see all of my sisters were there with Mary.

Dad was still hanging on, but he was not at peace. Faith knew what needed to be done. We needed to let him go. We all went into Dad's room and sat on his bed. Faith said, "Dad, all of us girls are here with you, and Mary too. I just connected with Kenny and we all want you to know that we love you. But if there are people calling to you—your parents, your brothers, and our mother—go to them, you should go. We will all be together again, Dad. You, us, and Mary. We love you, Dad." He then took his last breath. It was heart-wrenching and beautiful.

"An Olde Irish Toast" was never more important than it was that Sunday morning. We truly believe Dad was in heaven an hour before the devil knew he had died. I, too, needed to clear my head and heart. I went for a run around the Hospice compound and put on my headphones and listened to Kris Kristofferson's "Sunday Mornin' Comin' Down" over and over again until I found the courage to go back and prepare myself for a very long, very sad time. During that run, I remember thinking I wished I had been closer to Dad. I suppose we were as close as possible considering our family dynamics. There were just so many kids and his time was divided between all of us, his wife, and his many jobs. I got caught up in all the "if only's" and decided it would only drain me of all the strength I was going to need for my grieving family members. I felt that since I was the oldest, I needed to step up to the plate and be strong and focused for them. I was worried that if I fell apart then, I wouldn't get myself back together in time. I didn't allow myself to properly grieve Dad's passing until a couple of weeks later.

When I was finally able to come to terms with the fact that my Dad was gone, I was overcome with a sense of grief like I had never experienced before. I was so sad for our family that we lost the anchor of our lives. I also felt like I was abandoned. I had lost Mom 40 years before and now I had lost dad. I realized I was an orphan at the age 53.

THE PARTING GLASS

THERE WAS A two-day regular wake for Dad at a local funeral home. Hundreds of people came over the course of those two days. My sister Mary Grace collected any pictures we had of Dad. She made large poster board collages to put on easels in the middle of the funeral home. They were assembled in a long, two-sided row. People commented that they had never seen anything like it before. It was like you were walking around an art gallery admiring the beautiful pictures. The difference was, they were pictures of Dad with all his family and friends. To us, it was the most beautiful art we had ever seen; they were canvasses of Dad's life. Mary Grace also made a video that played for the duration of the wake. It was so odd to see him there, smiling and happy, only to look over and see him in his Irish green casket. We are not sure if the management of the funeral home knew we had a small Irish pub set up in a side room where drinks were abundant. And if they did know, they allowed us that indulgence. They were wonderful to us.

In his casket, people left little trinkets for him to be buried with. My sister Faith thought he needed something of Mom's. When she went home the night before his funeral, she found her cherished mustard seed ring. The next morning, she was able to get one of the people who worked there to open the casket quickly, so she could place the ring in his hands. Dad was then ready to enter the pearly gates and set his beautiful blue eyes on his Molly.

We had an over-the-top Irish wake for Dad. Our friends could not believe what a party it was. First, his funeral mass was at St. Stephen's Church on Grand Island. The Police Honor Guard was there, and I was filled with pride when they all stood at attention outside of the church. Their presence made me feel I was part of another family. I was the child of one of their own, and they were there to honor Dad. I again felt *bonded to the blue*.

After the mass, we all walked out across the parking lot onto the street and over to his burial site. I never witnessed anything like that before at a funeral. It reminded me of Irish movies I had seen where people follow behind the coffin. We had our very own version of an Irish funeral procession. It was a snowy, sleety day and very muddy. People didn't seem to mind that they were sinking into the ground as the priest said his final prayers. When the priest finished, we headed about a mile away to the restaurant we had chosen beforehand. There was a large buffet and, of course, an open bar. My cousin from out of town brought her violin and played some beautiful Irish songs while my nieces and I danced an Irish jig for Dad. I then recited "An Olde Irish Toast" and said just a few other words that came from my broken heart. We all clicked our *parting glasses* and said "Sláinte."

The most wonderful part of the day was when our last remaining sibling, Kenny, made it back home before the end of the Irish wake. He had been volunteering in Nepal, helping to build a classroom school out of earth bags in a remote village that was greatly affected by the earthquake. He learned of Dad's passing while he was there. He was able to get flights back to Buffalo, but his original flights were either cancelled or grounded. It took him two and a half days to get back. When he texted us that he would be arriving shortly, we all walked out of the restaurant to wait for him. We all actually cheered when he came walking towards us. Kenny looked a bit haggard from his long days of traveling, but he was smiling and seemed happy to be back home with all of us. He needed our embraces, which we all freely gave to him. There were tears, hugs, kisses, and sibling bonding. It was the most miraculous homecoming I have ever experienced. Dad now had all of his children there at his party. He could be at peace, and we felt he was definitely there in spirit.

As expected, after the wake and funeral were over, there were things to be taken care of. The siblings who were in town went over to our parents' home to help with the gathering, disbursement, and purging of his effects. Mary generously told us we could take things of Dad's that we wanted. I asked for his handcuffs and all of his ties. I took around thirty of them. I would give them to different siblings, family members, or friends when I felt they would be something someone would cherish. I also took his open bottle of English Leather aftershave. I liked knowing that he probably used it for the last time around the holidays when he was still able to dress himself. To this day when I am sad and missing him, I take a drop of his aftershave and put it on my wrist. I then feel I am connected to him in some small way by the scent.

My family and I all had to learn how to navigate through our lives without Dad. There were no more holidays shared with him, weekly gatherings, Last Suppers or even short phone calls to just say hello. I remember for the first year after his passing, I would call my parents' phone number and hope that Mary didn't answer the phone. That would mean it would go to voicemail and I could hear his voice on the recording. It was at least some way of still feeling his presence.

In 2018, my friend was having a book signing party for me at her house. She invited a special guest to the party. The gentleman's name was Joey Giambra. She told me that he was a local musician, playwright, actor, and producer and she thought I should meet him. When we started talking, he asked me if I was related to Frank Quinn. I told him I was his daughter and I asked him how he knew Dad. He explained that he and Dad had worked together on the BPD many years ago and were partners for a short period of time. A couple of my sisters were there, and we all sat at the table in awe of this interesting and talented man. He shared stories with us about Dad that were mostly comical. We never really thought of Dad as being funny, but Joey Giambra said he was quite a character and would always make him laugh. He said that he always remembered how Dad would giggle rather than actually laugh. It was wonderful to spend time with someone who could tell us so much about Dad that we never knew. It was a remarkable conversation that I will never forget.

Later that year, I went to an event that was being held for Joey Giambra's *Bread and Onions* at the Kavinoky Theatre. Before he went on stage, I gave him one of Dad's beautiful red ties. He took my hand, held it, and thanked me for the gift. He said, "Your dad was one of my favorite people." After Joey Giambra passed away in May of 2020, I read all the articles and tributes that set out to honor this accomplished man. There was one particular statement Joey Giambra made which spoke to my heart: "I've got my bag of souvenirs, leftover thoughts of yesteryears."[10] My Dad's ties, handcuffs, and aftershave are my souvenirs, leftover thoughts of his yesteryears.

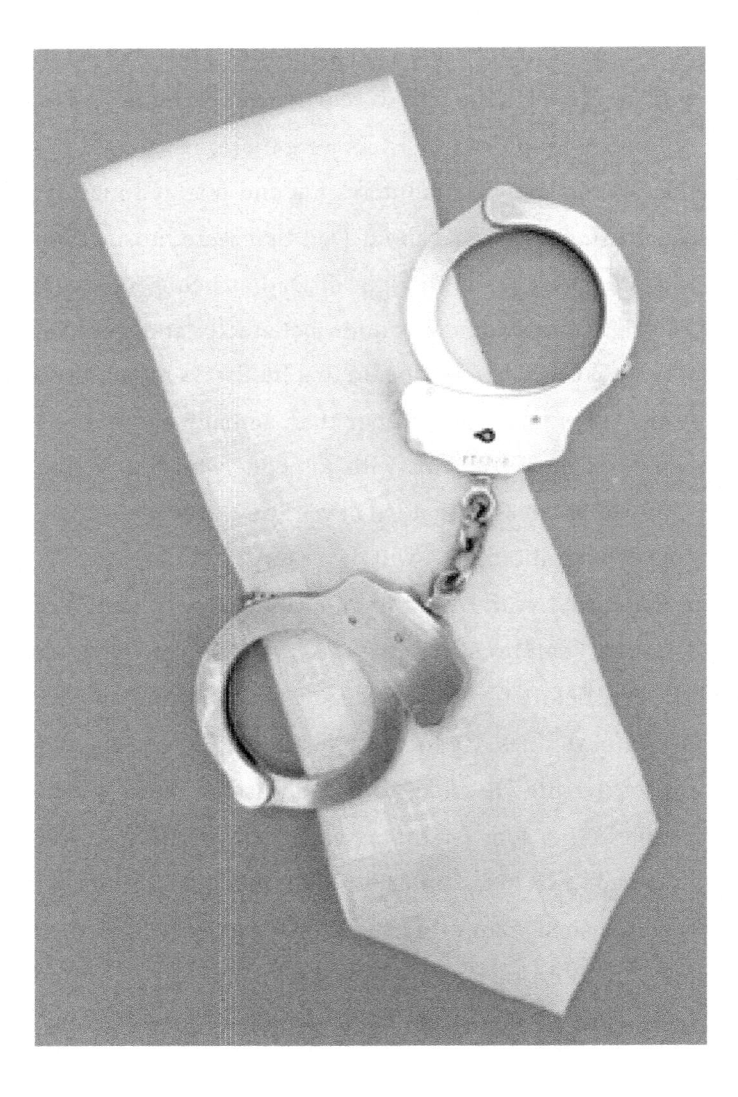

THE DANCE

EVEN THOUGH DAD is gone, we still continue to relive our memories of him. On the first Father's Day after his passing, my sister Faith put together what she called "The Frank Quinn Reality Tour." She found out things about Dad from when he was younger and decided we should go and revisit those places. She hired a bus and a driver to take us to places he went to when he was growing up. It was an awesome day.

We started off at South Buffalo Mercy Hospital where he was born. We then drove over to Pries Avenue and stood in front of the house he grew up in. To me, the house looked the same as it did the last time I visited our grandmother Julia there 20 years before. It was still the same light green color, and I walked around the side of the house to peek in the backyard. I let my mind go and pretended to see him up on the roof of his garage, his favorite hangout place when he was young.

We took photos of all our stops along the way. We ventured over to Holy Family Church where he was baptized, and then onto Bishop Timon High School where he graduated. From there we went to St. Theresa's Church on Seneca Street where he and Mom were married. In my mind's eye, I pictured Dad and Mom walking down the aisle of the church on their wedding day—he in his sharp white sports jacket and black bow tie suit and she with her beautiful, stylish wedding dress that ended just below the knee, showing off her shapely legs.

To me, the most memorable stop was the BPD's D District on Hertel Avenue. I felt so much pride in being a daughter of this accomplished police officer. We went in and explained to the report technician working at the desk why we were there. We looked around the small reception area, and back into the main room where we knew he would have walked through every day he reported to work there. I could picture him in his blue police uniform wearing his police jacket with the Buffalo police patch on the arm. My sister Kelly has his police jacket. Sometimes when I go to her house, I take it out of her closet and put it on. It feels somewhat like having his embrace.

We went back outside and lined up along the gate for a photo. Since I live in North Buffalo, back when Dad was alive, I would sometimes drive by him in his police car and nod to him and salute. I did the same that day when we were at the gate looking at all the police cars. To this day, every time I drive by a police car, I nod and salute.

Our last three stops were on Grand Island. We went to the little house on Redway Road where we spent the most time as a family, and then onto the house he lived in when he passed away. Our last stop was St. Stephen's Cemetery. We gathered around his grave and played our family song, "The Dance" by Garth Brooks, as we had done so many times in the past. We formed a circle around his headstone. We found peace and healing when we locked arms and swayed back and forth. To this day, my bond with my siblings has not been broken. The end to this perfect day for me was when I went to use the little bathroom that was on the bus. My sister Faith had made a paper copy of "An Olde Irish Toast" and taped it to the inside of the door. It was a very good Father's Day.

Every other year since Dad's passing, we have continued to have our family reunions. Lately, most of them have been done locally on Grand Island. We have one special "Frank Night" at the reunion. All of us wear a Hawaiian shirt (he loved them) or an actual shirt that he wore at one time. We have his favorite dinner of Bocce pizza and Oreo cookies for dessert. We listen to country music and play trivial pursuit. We talk about him fondly and listen to an actual recording of his voice that my sister Mary Grace saved on her phone. Without fail, we always play "The Dance" and do our family hand-holding or shoulder-locking sway for the duration of the song. We all feel the words sum up our life with Dad: "Our lives are better left to chance / I could have missed the pain / but I'd have to miss the dance."

MY WAY

DAD WAS A bit of a character. He had different endearing names for us. Some of them didn't make sense at all, but you felt lucky he thought enough about you to give you a nickname. Collectively he called us Dren Bastards. We assumed Dren was short for children, and although we knew we weren't bastards, he still called us all that. It was just his way. He was always giving us kids "wet willies." Dad would lick his finger and stick it in our ears. We all loved it when he did that. We felt it was his special connection to us. He had a quirkiness to him. For example, he wouldn't say the word ashtray but would instead say, "tray of asses." Instead of using the word car, he would say "Dren auto." He liked to put a spin on words and would sometimes use ones that didn't make sense but made us laugh. He just did things his own way.

Dad also had a unique way of being philosophical. I learned that he had a profoundly simple way of expressing his views all rolled into one statement and he shared it with people who were close to him. Some of those people still love to quote him to this day. It was, "It's all bull____!" When I asked my uncle what he thought that statement meant, he said, "Your Dad looked at things in an uncomplicated way and didn't want to get involved with the bull____. He had a realistic view of how things were and didn't want to be bombarded with needless bull____ that goes with it. Life is complicated enough, why add more bull____ to it."

I thought about his philosophy and realized that he was a man who did have a lot of bull____ thrown at him. But maybe he was able to deflect as much of it as possible by not allowing it to stick with him; it didn't penetrate or permeate his being. He just didn't have time in his life for nonsense and he did not want to deal with it or get involved in it. He liked to keep things simple – as simple as things could be in his complicated life.

I also recently learned that Dad did things his own way when it came to the issue of his dealing with all the parking tickets he accumulated for parking illegally around police headquarters while he was working there. It was assumed by some people that he was cheap or lazy and just didn't want to have to walk to and from one of the paid parking lots in the area. There was a church next door to Police Headquarters and several officers would park in front of it or behind the church. However, those spots were marked for no parking. Staff at the church would complain about all of the illegal parking to the Commissioner's Office. This resulted in numerous parking tickets being issued.

It touched my heart to find out that he told a friend that

the reason he was willing to accept this financial hardship of all of these tickets was that he always needed to have his car readily accessible to him in case he had to get home quickly. He always wanted to be available to our family if we needed him. Since I didn't learn this until after his passing, I felt a pang of sadness that I couldn't tell him how much this gesture meant to me. Again, it reinforces my belief that our family was everything to him. Although he couldn't say that to us as often as we would have liked to have heard, he proved it by having to pay large amounts of money for him to have a comfort level of knowing he could get to us if need be and quickly. I am not saying that I agree with his thought process on this matter. However, now every time I see a parking enforcement employee issuing a ticket for someone illegally parked, I smile and think to myself, "Thank you Dad. You really did love us. You just had a unique way of showing it."

He also did it his way when it came to dealing with the death of family and friends. I never thought about it until I was finalizing my memoir, but Dad did not feel comfortable around sick people. It could be the result of all the years he dealt with Mom's illness. I think he felt completely helpless in those situations and would avoid them if he could. However, he had a great reverence for people who had died. He would attend every wake for anyone he knew who had passed. He had the utmost respect for the dead.

I remember my sister Kelly sharing with me a tragic incident that happened in Mary's family. One of Mary's nieces was killed in a car accident. Kelly said things around their house were very quiet and solemn during that time; there was a feeling of despair in the air. Not many words were spoken, simply because no one knew what to say. Kelly said it was heartbreaking to her when Dad put his arms around her and just held her in a tight bear hug. He didn't say a word—just held on tight. He needed to comfort her, but also gain strength from the embrace. I think Dad knew how fortunate and blessed he was that he never had to see any of us kids pass away. As bad as things were with Mom's death, he found a way to deal with it. If he'd had to bury one of us, I don't believe he would have been able to handle that.

I was recently speaking with my cousin Julie who told me about a beautiful moment she shared with Dad. At his brother Bill's wake (Julie's father), she told me he said nothing, but unexpectedly embraced her in the warmest, kindest healing bear hug. She will never forget that moment with Dad. What Dad was not able to say in words to her, he was able to communicate through his bear hugs. Dad's childhood friend Jim shared with me that, at the same wake, Dad could not go up to the casket. He physically and emotionally could not do that. Of course, dealing with death is one of the most difficult things in life to do. Dad had to get through wakes the only way he could, but he made a point to be at them no matter how difficult it was.

When it came to his own death and facing his final curtain, Dad also did things his own way. Knowing that he would not want to linger on for years with cancer as our Mom did, he was able to go out on his own terms. I believe he felt it was necessary to get treatments for his disease to try and prolong his life. He didn't want to leave all of us. However, I think that when he saw the treatments were not working, he decided that he did not want to be sickly for years. It seems odd to say that I am glad he passed away relatively quickly; the time of his diagnosis to his death was only around six months. We were all able to spend the rest of the summer after his diagnosis with him around his pool. We continued our family get-togethers and went to Gene's vineyard in the fall. We all stopped in to see him on Thanksgiving and Christmas at his house. The 2016 New Year came and, shortly after that, he left us. And just as the song by Frank Sinatra goes, "And more, much more than this, I did it my way." Dad, too, *did it his way.*

THE MIGHTY QUINN

To honor Dad, "The Mighty Quinn" to all of us, our family still continues to go on the Buffalo Pedal Tour or Boat Tour every year. We wanted to continue this tradition even though he is no longer with us. We had life-size cardboard cutouts made of him and put his cutout likeness on the front of the bike or boat. When we get off at the different bars and other stops, we pick him up and bring him with us. People stare at us in amusement and amazement. Sometimes people even ask us why we have the poster board with us, and we all love to tell them the story of Dad. We have made so many connections to people on these ventures.

One of the greatest honors I believe Dad received after his passing was from his grandson, Jake, who had a tattoo of Dad's badge put on the back of his calf. When I asked him if he would tell me what inspired him to do that, he explained to me that he had always wanted to get a tattoo when he turned 18. He didn't know what it would be of, but he knew he would figure that out in time. After his Grandpa Quinn passed, he knew it was time and he knew what he was going to have tattooed onto his body. Jake said—

"Memories are great, and I have many wonderful memories of him. But I wanted something symbolic that would be forever indelible. To me, I always thought of his badge and what the badge means to our family. This was my way of honoring him and forever being connected to him."

I cried after Jake explained his thought process to me. But they were not sorrowful tears; rather, they were tears of pride. I thought how incredible it is that he would make such a grand gesture of dedication to his Grandpa Quinn. I also thought that Jake had developed a *bond of blue* in his own way. Jake's dad is also a retired police officer. I think Jake saw firsthand what it meant to be a child of someone who wears the blue and the sacrifices that go with that honor.

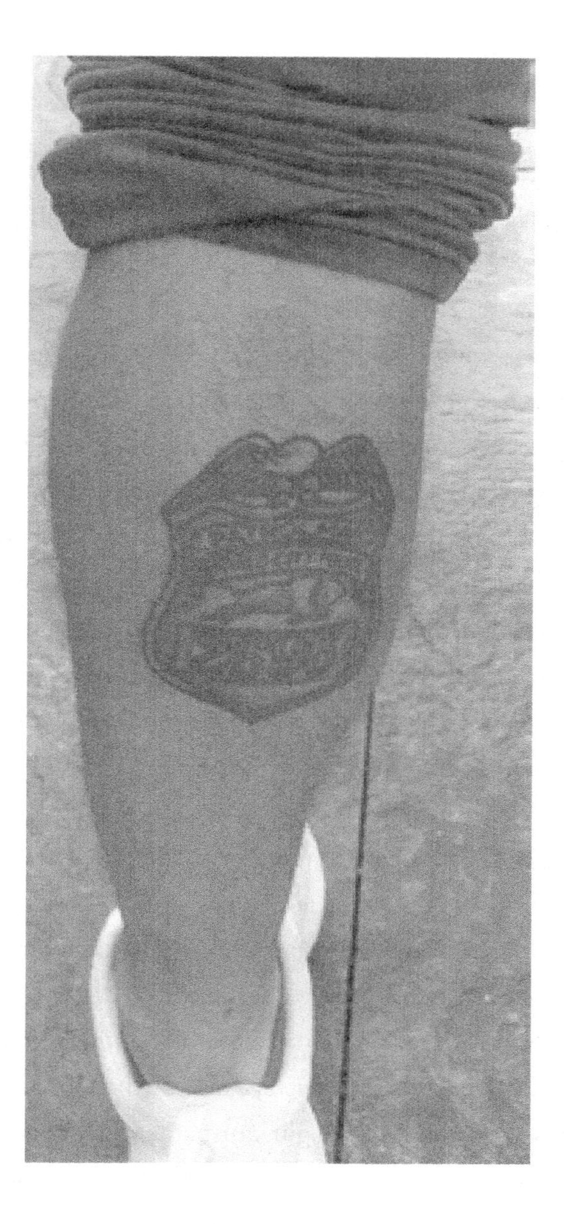

Every year on the anniversary of Dad's passing, we all honor him with a toast and have a Budweiser or a shot of Southern Comfort. After he first passed in 2016, my sister Kelly noticed a small, brown stink bug in her family's house. It just appeared out of nowhere and only stayed a few days. Stink bugs are known for emitting a pungent odor that smells like cilantro. They enter homes during the cooler winter months in search of a warm place.

I like to think that since Dad loved to go to their house when it was cold out and sit by the fireplace, he was making a special appearance at their warm home. They never noticed the bug smelled stinky. That only happens when the bug feels threatened in some way. Their stink bug would just walk around on the cupboards and floors, checking things out and hanging with their family. A stink bug usually appears at their house on the anniversary of "The Mighty Quinn's" passing. We believe he is there with us and always will be.

As I was finalizing my memoir, it just happened to coincide with the five-year anniversary of Dad's passing. I wanted to do something special with my family to commemorate this anniversary and just connect with them, share our stories and have our shots of Southern Comfort or a Budweiser. However, because of the Coronavirus, we were not able to have our normal family get-together with all of us who live locally. Our step-mother Mary was at St. Joseph's Hospital in Cheektowaga, NY which was turned into a hospital for people with Covid; she eventually recovered. Also, several family members were dealing with their own Covid issues and were in quarantine. I felt I just had to do something. Three days before the actual anniversary, I went to Bocce Pizza and bought pizzas for all of my sisters and their families who live in town. I also purchased bags of Oreo cookies and brought a bottle of Southern Comfort to his gravesite. While I was there, I placed a single white rose on his gravestone. I didn't sing or play the song "The Dance" as I would have done if I had my siblings around me. Without my family there with me, it seemed empty and too sad to even think of the words. Instead, I just offered up a little prayer for him and hoped he was at peace. Before leaving, I cleaned up the area around his grave that still had little trinkets my family left on Halloween and the wreath I left there for him at Christmas which I had all of our names put on. It was at that time, I realized how blessed I have been that I have had my family in my life to share the sadness and to help fill the void of Dad being gone.

I collected the pizzas, Oreos and the bottle of Southern Comfort and dropped individual packages of Dad's favorite treats at each sister's home. Sadly, that night when I returned home, I realized I forgot to get myself some pizza and Oreos. I was disappointed about that but I at least I had the Southern Comfort to drink that night when I got home! On the actual anniversary date of January 10, my siblings and I all shared texts and photos of Dad. It helped us to get through the day. I called my sister Kelly and asked her if she saw a stink bug that day. She told me that she saw a stink bug around her house for around a month, but not on that day. I was saddened by that. However, I remember learning that the last stage of grief is acceptance. I like to think that Dad had been there to let us know he would always be around to help us get through our grief. But now, maybe he doesn't need to be since he knows we have reluctantly accepted his passing and are moving forward in our lives. He knows we all carry him in our hearts.

GREATER THAN ALL MY REGRETS

One of the regrets I have concerning Dad is that I never asked him questions about his father. It wasn't until I read all of the astounding newspaper articles about my grandfather that I understood how much he was revered and respected in his community. I never met my paternal grandfather, as he passed away the year before I was born. I only recently found out about a couple that he and my grandmother Julia were best friends with. They would go to each other's homes to play cards and have dinners. I was taken aback to learn that I actually live in the same house that this couple lived in back in the 50s and 60s in North Buffalo. It was heartening to know that my grandfather actually had wonderful times in my house with his friends. I also learned that my grandfather liked to drink hot tea. As I was writing my memoir in the computer room of my house, I would sip at a cup of hot tea. It made me feel connected to my grandfather, and I felt his presence every step of the way. I also kept a bottle of Southern Comfort with me, but I only had a swig of that in the evenings. Of course, that made me feel close to Dad.

I also regret that I never thanked Dad for all of the sacrifices he made to keep our family together. Had he not done that for all of my siblings and me, this story would not have been told. I recently spoke with my brother Christian, who was the third youngest in our family hierarchy. He never realized the extent of what Dad went through after our mother passed. He was too young to have a memory of how things were for all of us before that. After he read a draft of my memoir, he had a better understanding and appreciation of Dad. For me, knowing that I have given my siblings and family members a greater insight into this simply complex man is a gift. Perhaps I have helped to heal other's wounds. What I hope I have accomplished is *greater than any of my regrets.*

We all get so caught up in our lives. We don't seem to find the time to sit down with our loved ones when they are with us to ask them questions about their upbringings, their hopes, or their dreams. We lose touch with aunts, uncles, cousins, etc. Another gift that has come out of writing this story is that I have connected with family members I have not communicated with in many years. I too believe in *family above all.*

When I decided to do this tribute to Dad it took me in different directions. It has been a work in progress and a labor of love. Every night that I sat at my computer putting my thoughts into words, it was reflective, uplifting, and heartbreaking. I would reread what I had written about all of these memories and stories of Dad. It was like ripping a band-aid off of a wound over and over again. Most families do have it hard. This was just our hard. But in retrospect, you have to have an open wound for the healing to begin. That is where I am at now.

If I had the opportunity to go back and do it over again, I would have taken the time to share with Dad how proud I was of him and all his accomplishments. Unfortunately, that is not possible. So, the next best thing I could do to pay tribute to him is to share this story. I now have peace.

I love you Dad.

EPILOGUE

It all was and still is, bittersweet. But our family has continued to grow. As of this memoir, our Quinn family has grown to: Mary Pierre; Frank (father to Amelia "Molly," Frank, Zachary, Nicholas, and Larry; grandfather to Marshall, James, Elijah and MiKenzie); Kim; Faith (mother to Amelia, Christian, and Jacob; grandmother to Mason); Kenneth; Joseph; John (father to Sarah and Joshua); Christian (father to Faith); Mary Grace (mother to Ashley, Aubree, Alicia, Aaron, and Aerik); and Kelly (mother to Noah and Ella).

Beyond my father's children, our extended family includes my uncle William, father to three and grandfather to one; my aunt Maryellen, mother to three and grandmother to nine; and my uncle Thomas, father to two and grandfather to one.

Their legacy lives on.

FRANCIS P. QUINN'S EULOGY

WRITTEN AND PRESENTED by John Arnone

Frank Quinn was a great man, I think we can all agree, who deserves a great send-off, delivered by a great speaker. Unfortunately, you will be hearing from me… I'm sorry Frank…

I am both honored and overwhelmed to have been asked to speak for the family as we remember Francis – Frank, as we all knew him.

I am John Arnone, husband to Kelly, the youngest of Frank's children. I too am in many ways the youngest member of this family. I met Kelly in 2002 which makes me—perpetually—the new guy. So from time to time, over the past 14 years, I have had the impossible task of describing the Quinns to my friends and family. You find yourself at a loss for words but compelled to try to explain just how connected, functional, loving, inspiring, welcoming, and remarkable this family really is. It is a relief to look around this room and know that I will not have to do that today. You're here today because you all know exactly what I mean. You have all been touched by his family in some way. You have been blessed with their massive, radiating, all-encompassing gravitational pull, and the way you are made to feel when you have been in the company of the Quinns.

At the center of this amazing family, of course was Frank Quinn—father of ten. Just let that set in for a moment… father of ten children. I have two children and I can barely get out of bed in the morning. If the story ended here, it would be remarkable enough. But he was also grandfather of 18, great-grandfather, husband, brother, father-in-law, brother-in-law, uncle, police officer, partner, babysitter, horrible joke teller, Hawaiian-shirt-wearer, Southern Comfort drinker, serial tanner, proud Irishman, and an irreverent rule breaker, with no regard for decorum or authority. A man who recently tried to bring a handgun into a Sabres' game.

As the family navigated the last few days, I was able to ask them about Frank and what they wanted mentioned here. So, with all of his children, Mary, his grandchildren, close friends, family, and in-laws I was afraid that it would be impossible to gather all of those thoughts and memories. But as I collected ideas, my job was made simple. The same sentiments came out with each person. He was a selfless, humble man. A man so humble, in fact, that he would change out of his uniform before he stopped at the store because he didn't want special treatment. He was a dedicated, giving father who never let the burden of his misfortunes touch his children. Quinn after Quinn told story after story of a man who endured heartache and loss only to put his children before himself. He made it his life's mission to keep his children together; each sacrifice revealed a kindness and love so deep that it became his legacy. He never had to say a word, never had to shed a tear, raise his voice in anger or break down in defeat. Yet, he must have felt like doing all of those things at times.

The other sentiment echoed over the years was that his children wished that there were more words from Frank. He was a man of few words: simple yet complicated, as he has been described. He said very little, and everyone wanted to know what was going on beyond the constant smile and laughing eyes. What was he really thinking? Those long silences made him such a mystery to us all because we wondered how he managed to come through it with such grace, humor, and dignity.

I'm not sure if those who loved Frank could ever know what was really going on inside, what he would have said if he could. But I feel that you all speak for him, from him, through him. You are all Frank Quinns. He gave you the words that you express so beautifully, and he never had to say them. The Quinns are funny, intelligent, strong-willed, and loyal. As Cowboy likes to say, "cut one and they all bleed." They are powerful, infinitely positive, and absolutely selfless. They are nurses, teachers, businessmen, first responders, firemen, social workers, builders and fixers, miracle workers, wish granters, writers and philosophers, explorers and humanitarians—caregivers all…

Each in his and her own way say the words that Frank never said, never had to say: I see you. I care about you. I hear you. I'm here for you. I think about you. I'm worried about you. I think you're right. I'm proud of you. I know you're going to be alright… and, of course, the words that I did hear him say out loud, every day to each of you: "I love you."

The story of the Quinns, Frank, and the family, has never ceased to amaze me. Each time we get together and as most of you know, the Quinns get together… a lot. You know this if you've been around. A spontaneous, 20-person house party can materialize out of nowhere, without warning. Kelly will quietly mention, "Oh, my sister might be dropping by…" and bam, you're drinking with the family until 2am… and it's a Monday.

However, each time we get together, I hear a story that I've never heard before. And it is a testament to his family, to Mary, that those stories always include Molly. For 14 years, Frank and Molly built the foundation to this mansion, this castle, the cathedral that would become the Quinn family. Some have vivid memories of their mother while for others, her memory has been shaped by the love that still radiates from her time with us. When they paint a picture of Molly for us, she is angelic—fighting for her life, but still so beautiful through their eyes that we are sorry that we never met her. But of course, we knew her… She is Mary Pierre, Frankie, Kimmy, Faith, Kenny, Joey, Johnny, Christian, and Mary Grace. She lives in all of you, and you have surely passed her down to your children.

And the story continues… In 1978, Frank married Mary Lipiec… I need to note here that this is a family (grandchildren included) of over 30 people, but there are only about eight different names. There are multiple Franks, Christians, Mollys, Faiths, and everyone else is named Mary. So Frank and Mary began their life together with challenges that few would face. Nine children, the financial concerns that came with that, and the difficult work of healing. Nine children… From what I understand this was not a secret. Mary knew this… if you can believe that. It's not like Frank hid seven of them in the basement and said, "Did I forget to mention that I have nine children?" And Mary took this on. The children told me of the sacrifices Mary made for them, that they were always cared for and that she made sure they always got the Christmas gift they wanted. They also talked about how much she doted on Frank. Frank always said, "It's better to look good than it is to feel good." And Frank always looked good, because Mary ironed every outfit, shopped tirelessly, made sure he had a fresh supply of band-aids, and stocked up on whatever the hell that stuff was he put in his hair. She made sure he was cared for. Mary never set foot in a pool, but she made sure Frank always had a clean pool to enjoy every summer. And, of course, as Johnny said, "If not for Mary, we would not have our little sister, Kelly." Kelly, who has been treated like one of the pack since day one.

And then came the grandchildren. Frank was such a proud grandfather, and he must have felt as if they gave him another chance at missed opportunities because I can tell you that he never missed an opportunity with his grandchildren. I knew he loved them all equally, but there was a special place in Frank's heart for the two-year-olds. He was generous with his time, and he showed them each how much he loved them even if his grandparenting skills were questionable. He loved to tease and taunt them. His eyes lit up when they rushed into the room, and he would stick his finger in their ears or bait them mercilessly and then tell them to stop being whiners. He liked to treat them like house-cats with his laser pointers; he relished their bickering, saying that dissent was good for them. "Children, fight nicely," he would say with a giggle. He tossed them in the pool and shared his cashews with them. He rolled his eyes at their drama and laughed at their frustrations. He caught them when they fell and teased them some more. But he never once lost his temper. I watched him care lovingly for my own children, and I could not thank him enough for the hours he spent babysitting and the many, many sleepovers when he gave up his peace and quiet for chaos.

I could go on for hours about Frank, a man I came to see as a second father and a dear friend. So many of you sent me thoughts and ideas—I want to thank you, and I hope I did justice to the memory of your father.

But Frank wouldn't approve of a morose, overly sentimental send-off. I can see him rolling his eyes now. So I collected a list of people and places and things that I hope will bring a smile to your face. As I share this with you, please laugh out loud, poke each other, hug each other, embrace, shake hands, nod your head, cry... whatever. But let's try to create the noise and chaos that was music to Frank's ears.

There were Frankisms: Milsh, Walter, Auto, Dren-Bastards, Dicko, Leaky, Nick Nick, Juda, Indeed, Perhaps-perchance.

Bocce Pizza, ½ boxes from Bocce Pizza, prime rib, cheeseburgers and chocolate monkeys, macadamia nuts, pepperoni, pudding, Chiavetta's, hidden chocolates and Chinese food, room temperature Budweiser and Southern Comfort...

The Bonaire, The Royal Pheasant, Casa D'Ora, Swiss Chalet, Chicken Galore, South Buffalo, Happy Jacks, Las Vegas, Canada, Gene's Farm, Sibley's, The Whistle Pig,

Pries Avenue, Tom's beach house, LaHacienda, Lake Erie State Park, hours around the kitchen table. Wayne Newton, Robert Goulet, Clark Gable, Elvis, The Police Commissioner. Something about a phone call to the Police Commissioner?

As seen on TV stuff, foot rubs, the two times he tried to ride a bike, our bike ride downtown last year, wet willies, TPU, Precinct 13, Precinct 11, Badge #2696, parking tickets, WECK Radio, Walmart, 65" TV, the Pink Gremlin, burned out light bulbs, indoor extension cords (out of doors), mint-green spearmint candles, "The Wreck of the Edmund Fitzgerald," constantly crashed computers, beta tapes, whatever he recorded over VHS tapes, lost handguns, bobble heads, baseball and left-handers, pool floats and chlorine, crushed ice, that year-round tan, Members Only Jackets, Trivial Pursuit, Pinochle, laser pointers, The Fireman's Carry, hours of rooftop at Pries Avenue, driving 100 miles per hour in the Chevy Impala, Little Frankie at the pool and more Trivial Pursuit.

He was Quinny, Giggles, The Suit and Butch...

Frank left us Sunday surrounded by his girls and Mary. He was a guy's guy, as they say...but it was the girls who opened him up to the world. It was only fitting that they were there to pass him back to Molly.

I said earlier that Frank's words were precious few, but the words he did share had tremendous impact. I was working on this and I got stuck. I didn't know how I could end this, and I was sort of talking out loud to Frank while I was staring at the blank page, when a text came through from Johnny. He had found a handwritten letter from his father, penned 24 years ago. I read it and the tears started streaming down my face. As if on cue, Frank sent us down the only words that will ever really matter.

I leave you with what he sent to Johnny, in a letter dated January 13, 1992. He writes in his closing… "I hope to see you soon because I really miss you and Joe. I know that I am not a very affectionate person but believe me, the most important thing in my life are my ten children. I know I don't really express my affection for you and your brothers and sisters but believe me, I love you all very much."

Frank…you will be deeply missed.

AFTERWORD

When I originally stared out writing my memoir, I had planned to call it "The Band of Blue." However, with each chapter I was writing, it became clear to me that there was an actual bond between my father, his father, several family members, friends and all of the men and women who are in law enforcement. It is a bond that does not seem to be able to be broken.

The decision for the book's title was solidified after I had a conversation with my Uncle Richard. I was asking him questions about Dad as he had a relationship with him since he was my mother's brother. He shared stories with me about Mom and Dad's courtship years which I have shared in a previous chapter. However, what really captured my attention was when he told me a story about how it was that he came to be in law enforcement. He was a young man who had just gotten out of the Marines and was looking for a direction in his life. One day he was speaking with my Mom and Dad about going out to California to find a job. My Mom convinced Dad to reach out to family that he had in California on Richard's behalf. Uncle Richard hit the big time when he was hooked up with my Dad's uncle, Joseph M. Quinn who was the Deputy Mayor of Los Angeles at the time. Joe Quinn was also the former Los Angeles Press Club president, a veteran journalist, war correspondent and past editor of City News Service. He and his family generously offered to have Richard come and stay in their beautiful home in the Los Feliz area of LA. They lent him a Pontiac Firebird car for him to use while he was there looking for a job, provided him with groceries and with contacts with the LA Sheriff's Department. It wasn't long after Richard's initial visit to California that he was able to join the ranks of the LA Sheriff's Department. This was another family *bond of blue* connection that developed and changed the lives of many people. Richard's son, then followed his father into policing and is a Captain with the Los Angeles Sheriff's Department. The *bond of blue* runs deep and is continuously on-going. Therefore, the title "The Bond of Blue" was the obvious choice for the title of this book.

I will not even pretend that I can understand this special cohesion that the men and women of law enforcement seem to share. I am just so honored and privileged that I played some small role in this special connection, and more importantly, that I come from a family of blue.

Again, I thank all who are in law enforcement for your courage and fortitude that you show every day on the job.

If it were not for your dedication to all of the communities throughout our nation, we would not have the security we have in our lives. You all are truly heroes.

PART 2

Fictional Story

INTRODUCTION

I HAVE ALWAYS had a fascination with true crime novels and television shows. After I read the 180 newspaper articles that my grandfather, Frank P. Quinn, was referenced in from his time with the BPD (1939 – 1962), I felt he was a true-life Dick Tracy. Dick Tracy was a comic strip featuring a tough, incorruptible, plainclothes detective who was relentless in pursuing criminals. My grandfather actually resembled Dick Tracy in some of the pictures from these articles with his dark suit, white shirt, necktie, and a fedora hat. He also had the same persistence to solve crimes.

One small article, in particular, captured my heart and attention more than the others. It was about the homicide of an infant boy in 1946. I named the baby "Danny Boy." Having learned from family members and neighborhood friends how much family meant to my grandfather, the little boy's death must have been something that stayed on his mind. I couldn't help but think that my grandfather must have been searching for answers to this unresolved case. In the absence of any closure to the actual case, my mind took me in the direction of a crime- solving sleuth. Since my grandfather couldn't solve "Danny Boy's" murder, I thought of a way to fictionally do it for him by telling this story of what might have been...

And perhaps-perchance, with divine intervention and good old-fashioned police work, this very cold case could someday, possibly, be unfrozen.

WHAT MIGHT HAVE BEEN

FRANK P. QUINN joined the BPD in 1939 as a Patrolman. He had an exceptional career in the department and earned numerous promotions. At various times throughout his career, he was assigned to different stations and squads under various Police Commissioners. In 1946 when he was a Detective, there was one case that he was involved in that forever changed him. It was the murder of a newborn baby that he and his partner responded to.

The infant was found on the ice of Scajaquada Creek near the West Avenue Bridge. It was something that shook him to his core. Frank never shared this information with his family. It was heart-wrenching to him. He would look at his beautiful wife and four children every night and thank God for how blessed he was. He never wanted them to know how heavy his heart felt when he first saw the little boy's lifeless body in the bag. Family was everything to him, and he couldn't imagine how someone could harm an innocent infant. This little boy's death haunted him. He felt that until he was able to solve the crime and know the circumstances surrounding this little boy's death, he would not be at peace.

Frank was moving up in the BPD. In 1949, he was assigned to the Chisholm Murder case and ultimately assisted in solving the crime. This brought him favorable attention by the department brass and the public. He and his partner were honored by the Retail Liquor Stores Association of Western New York. They were presented with diamond rings set in onyx. Frank was honored and humbled to be presented the beautiful ring. He planned to someday pass it down to one of his sons.

Body of Baby Found in Bag

The body of a newly-born baby boy was found late yesterday afternoon in a black cloth zipper bag on the ice of Scajaquada Creek near the West Ave. bridge. The body was wrapped in a Sunday edition of a New York newspaper.

Homicide squad detectives said Gordon Willard, 16, of 376 Dewitt St. and two companions made the discovery while playing on the creek bank.

"We saw the bag on the thin ice and wondered how it got there," young Willard related. "One of the smaller boys, Robert Demming, slid out on the ice and pulled the bag to shore. Then I opened it and called police."

Detectives John J. Foy, Frank P. Quinn and John P. Reville investigated at the scene and accompanied the infant's body to the morgue.

Dr. Paul J. Rutecki, medical examiner, will investigate the case. Dr. Harold J. Welsh, county pathologist, will perform an autopsy today.

Frank's career continued to advance through the mid-1950s and early 1960s. At one point, he was Head of the District A Squad in South Buffalo. His job was fulfilling, and his family life was even more rewarding. His children were growing up so quickly and he realized they would eventually be leaving their family home to start their own families.

One evening after dinner, Frank and his son Butch went out to throw the baseball around. That night, Butch told his father that he wanted to become a police officer and join the BPD. Frank had always hoped that one of his sons would follow in his footsteps, but he never wanted to badger them into making that decision. He felt that to be a good police officer, the desire had to come from within. It shouldn't be forced onto someone. From that evening on, a special bond developed between father and son. Frank's heart swelled with pride that Butch wanted to follow him into police work. It was that moment when Frank decided he would leave his prized onyx ring to Butch upon his passing. To Frank, the ring would solidify their *bond of blue.*

They both knew it would take a couple of years before this could happen. Butch would have to first graduate from high school. He would then have to take the Police Civil Service Test and score high enough to pass; Butch would have to follow all the proper procedures to get into the

BPD. When Butch told Frank of his intent to join the BPD, Frank felt like he could finally share his story of the baby boy's murder back in 1946. He told of how it was the most upsetting day he had ever had as a police officer, and about his disappointment in not being able to find out how this little boy had died. After telling the story, he and Butch would discuss it every time they saw each other. Frank told Butch that he named the deceased child "Danny Boy." It was his way of making a connection to the child since Frank's favorite song was "Danny Boy." The child and the way he died were forever on his mind and heart.

A couple of years later, Frank was on disability from the BPD due to a leg injury he had sustained while on the job earlier that summer. He liked to pass the time by sitting on his front porch, listening to Irish music drifting through the windows of the house. One evening, Butch and Frank were sharing a beer on the porch. Butch told Frank that he had been thinking a great deal about Danny Boy. He also said that if he were to get on to the BPD, he would want to someday be able to assist with solving the murder of the infant boy. At that point, he felt he could make a promise to Frank which he would try to keep. He said, "Dad, I know how much solving the case of Danny Boy would mean to you. Since I may one day be joining the ranks of the BPD, I will help you put some closure to the little boy's death. This is my promise to you, and I will do my best to keep it."

Unfortunately, Frank passed away in 1962 before he could see Butch join the BPD. Butch was devastated by his father's passing, but he knew he had to carry on and start his career. He had recently been married to a young woman named Molly and they hoped to be starting their own family. He had many things on his plate, but he was haunted by his father's torment of not being able to solve Danny Boy's murder. Even though his father was gone, he was more determined than ever to keep the promise he made regarding Danny Boy. He wanted to do this for his father's memory and his own peace. In 1966, four years after Butch's father had passed, he was hired by the BPD as a Patrolman.

Many years went by and Butch was doing well with the department. He had received promotions throughout his career and at one point he was a Detective with both the Special Frauds and the Narcotics Units. Butch and Molly had created a large family that continued to grow. As a result, he also worked a couple of part-time jobs to help make ends meet. However, Danny Boy and his promise to his father were never far from his thoughts.

As Butch's career was advancing with the BPD, his family life was in chaos. Molly had been diagnosed with lung cancer. She fought the disease for several years before she passed away in 1976. Her passing took a toll on Butch and his family. Although he still thought about the promise he made to his father, he had to put it out of his mind and focus on the needs of his family.

Butch was fortunate to find love again. In 1978, he married a young woman named Mary and they were blessed to bring another child into their family. He continued working for the BPD for the next 16 years. His family life was stable and most of his children had moved out and were starting their own families. He was proud of what he accomplished while working for the BPD, but with retirement only three years away, his thoughts returned to Danny Boy. He was finally in a place in his life where he could devote some time to keep the promise he made to his father over 30 years ago.

DANNY BOY

After gaining departmental permission to open and assist in the investigation of the cold case of Danny Boy, Butch had to start at the beginning and piece together the events that led up to the baby's death. The first thing he did was talk to the "old-timers" in the department to see what they remembered. He also began to search for police files on the case. He enlisted the help of his longtime friend Michele, a civilian employee of the BPD, to assist in researching the recorded history of the cold case. Since they both had children, the unsolved case created a special bond between them. They did not want to stop working the case until the homicide was solved.

It was late in 1994 when Michele started looking through old newspaper articles from 1946. She knew the approximate year to look for; Butch had given her all the information he could remember from conversations he'd had with his father. She went to the Buffalo History Museum and looked through many old articles that were on microfiche. She found the article "Body of Baby Found in Bag," as well as a second article from *The Buffalo Courier-Express* titled "Enquiry Continues in Baby's Death." She brought all of this information to Butch.

He then asked the detectives who were assigned to the cold case to take a fresh look in the evidence box that contained all of the material from the original investigation, and the original autopsy report. Fortunately, the box was still in the evidence room of Police Headquarters on Franklin Street. In the box, there were the yellowing, out-of-town newspapers that the baby had been wrapped in; the box also held the black zipper bag that the baby had been found in by boys playing on Scajaquada Creek. In 1946 when the infant was originally found, the BPD had been able to lift fingerprints off of the black zipper bag since it was not submerged in water. They also obtained fingerprints from a railing on top of the bridge after seeing the condition of the infant's body.

The officers—including Butch's father—may have assumed the person who threw the baby down onto the creek could have touched the railing. Back then, the BPD did not have a database that could be used to compare the prints. However, there were photographs of the fingerprint cards in the evidence box with prints on them and they were able to run the old prints through the State's Fingerprint Identification System. With advancements in technology, when the detectives ran the prints on the cards, they received a hit! The fingerprints belonged to Antonino Gaeta.

Now that the detectives had a name, they were able to

further investigate Antonino Gaeta in their data systems. They discovered that until four months ago, Gaeta had been in Attica prison serving a sentence for illegal gambling and violating the conditions of his parole from the Clinton Correctional Facility. He had served time there until 1992 for committing statutory rape back in 1950. Unfortunately, it also showed that their prime suspect was deceased. The detectives realized they would never be able to prosecute Antonino Gaeta for the death of the infant in 1946. However, that did not stop them from wanting to obtain as much information as they could on this murderer.

They came to learn that Antonino "Tony" Gaeta was originally a small-time offender. The detectives working the case were able to locate Gaeta's former wife, and she was only too happy to share information with them. He had a few minor arrests for illegal gambling but was able to hire top-notch attorneys for those charges. The attorneys were able to circumvent him having to spend time in prison for any of the charges associated with illegal gambling. However, Gaeta didn't have the same monetary resources as he had in the past when he was arrested and charged with statutory rape in 1950. He was sentenced to serve 20 years in the Clinton Correctional Facility for this crime. The records also showed that he had extra time added onto his sentence for a crime he was involved in while he was in that prison.

It took another month of searching but Butch, Michele, and the detectives from the cold case squad were ultimately able to put together enough evidence to bring some closure to the case. They were able to figure out the who, what, where, and when. This was far more information than they had ever expected to find, but they had no way to figure out the why. No way, that is, until a break in the case came from a very unexpected source. The detectives had an incredible stroke of luck, and perhaps divine intervention played a role when they got a break in the case.

In 1995, four months after the closure of the Danny Boy case, one of the detectives who worked on the cold case received a call from the captain at the A District, otherwise known as the South District in Buffalo, NY. Apparently, the captain had been contacted by a Sister Rita from the Sisters of Mercy on Abbott Road and she asked to talk to the appropriate authorities about the murder of an infant boy back in 1946. Though he wasn't familiar with the case, the captain took down Sister Rita's phone number and told her he would call her back with the name and phone number of the correct authorities.

The detective couldn't believe what he was hearing. Since Sister Rita knew the exact year that the infant died, she must be referring to Danny Boy. None of the information the BPD had recently obtained regarding the case was ever released to the newspapers or media, so she must have had firsthand knowledge. The detective asked the captain for her phone number and told him he would call the woman back himself.

He phoned Sister Rita back immediately. It was a very brief call just to set up a time to come to the convent and talk with her in person. When the detective hung up with her, he tried to call Butch to share this information but was unable to reach him. After all, Butch was the main reason the case had been reopened in the first place. He thought to see if Michele would be willing to go with him to see Sister Rita, to help put the nun at ease. Luckily, Michele was working at Police Headquarters, and was more than happy to accompany the detective!

The detective and Michele drove over to the Sisters of Mercy Convent as soon as they could. The nun who answered the door introduced herself as Sister Rita. After introducing themselves, Sister Rita invited them to sit in the parlor area of the convent. She explained to them that a few months ago, a priest from the Attica area came to her with some disturbing information. He told her that he had heard the confession of a dying prisoner named Antonino Gaeta and that Gaeta had shared a great deal of information with him about his life of crime. Gaeta needed to unburden his soul.

Due to the priest's obligation to uphold the confidentiality of the information he heard during a sacramental confession, he would not go to the police with the knowledge he obtained from Gaeta. He further went on to explain that the man asked him to pass along information to a woman named Darlene Dolan, who had worked at a bar in South Buffalo's Old First Ward back in the 1940's. He wanted to tell Darlene that he was sorry for what he did to her baby. The priest also told Sister Rita that Gaeta wouldn't stop talking about all of his other past sins, and about his life in general. Since most of what he said was outside of his confession, the priest shared the information with Sister Rita. Both Sister Rita and the priest believed Gaeta was telling the truth. At that point in his life, there was no reason for him not to. He was a dying man who was speaking his last truth.

Sister Rita's voice then started to quiver just a bit. She took a couple of deep breaths and said to them, "I have a confession to make. What I am about to tell you I have already confessed to my Lord and Savior, and God has forgiven me. I just have not been able to forgive myself. I feel that until I unburden myself by telling you my story, I will not have peace. I want to include information that Gaeta shared with the priest who came to me, as that information fills in some of the holes in my story." She told them that it could take a while for her to get through the story as she felt she needed to start at the very beginning. They told her to take all the time she needed.

Sister Rita started by telling them that she knew Darlene Dolan. Darlene was a very pretty girl with a beautiful, bright smile. But she was lonely and burdened with a great deal of family responsibility. Darlene knew she wanted a better life for herself; she dreamed of a way out from the monotony of her everyday life. Darlene was born in 1930 to Angela and Jimmy Dolan who were both born and raised in Buffalo. Her father, Jimmy, was not an ambitious man, doing just enough to get by. His father, Seamus Dolan had willed his bar—Dolan's—to Jimmy.

There was one stipulation in the will: if Seamus were to pass, Mabel, the head bartender, would take over management of Dolan's. Seamus knew that Jimmy would run Dolan's into the ground, and he couldn't bear to think of that. Mabel was skilled in cooking, bookkeeping, ordering, and some nursing. Seamus recognized her abilities. Mabel had gone to school for nursing but had gotten involved with the wrong crowd. She never was able to receive her actual nursing credentials. Still, locals came to her for minor medical treatments. She would sometimes tend bar and stitch up a cut of a patron who got into a scuffle, all in the same night. Mabel was a woman of many hats who worked hard to make Dolan's the place the locals wanted to go to, and it was doing well enough to provide for the Dolan family.

Unfortunately, Seamus was killed near the end of Prohibition. A young man came into Dolan's and shot Seamus through his heart. The shooter was never caught. The word on the street was that Seamus was perceived as a threat to the other bootleggers in the area, and they wanted him removed from the lucrative competition. Not long after, Prohibition ended, and Dolan's was doing well financially. It was Mabel's many years of working at Dolan's and her astute business practices that were the main reason for the bar's success.

Mabel started noticing that the men who came into Dolan's would constantly ask about Darlene, so when Darlene turned sixteen, Mabel had her start tending bar. She first made sure that Jimmy didn't have a problem with his daughter bartending. At that time, it was unusual to have a young woman working at the bar. However, many of the patrons of the establishment were police officers and firemen, so Darlene felt safe. It was a tight-knit community; everyone looked out for each other, and they looked out for Darlene. Mabel made sure that either she or Jimmy were always at Dolan's when Darlene was tending bar. Mabel thought of her as the daughter she never had. They developed a friendship and Darlene was closer to Mabel than to her own mother.

The business was booming with Darlene behind the bar, but she had a great deal on her plate. She attended

South Park High School during the day and then would go home and take care of her younger siblings before heading to the bar, sometimes working until closing. She also attended mass every Sunday and on Holy Days of Obligation. She was a devout Catholic and her faith and church were very important to her.

Not long after she started tending bar, Darlene met Antonino Gaeta. He went by the name of Tony, and he was very good looking. The night they met, Tony and his friends were out celebrating his big win from the previous night's poker game. They were downtown living it up at the Town Casino. Since the Casino was closing for the night, they wanted a place to go to continue partying. One of the fellows said he knew of a place over in the First Ward where the drinks were cheap and served until 3 am. They made their way over to Dolan's.

They were not disappointed when they stumbled in to find that the bar was still crowded and there was popular music being played on the jukebox. They were a boisterous group, flashing cash like Darlene and her father had never seen. Drinks were flowing, people were dancing, and Tony couldn't take his eyes off of the young woman who had just served him a beer. Darlene kept her composure as she always did, but her heart felt a pang that night when he handed her a fifty- dollar bill and told her to keep the change. She was embarrassed that she couldn't look him straight in the eye; she felt like a bolt of lightning was going through her body. She had never felt that way before, but it happened that night, and it didn't stop until around nine months later.

Tony and Darlene started a one-way love affair. They would meet as often as he was able to find the time for her. He would pick her up a few streets away from Dolan's and drive over to Cazenovia Park where they could be alone. He would tell her he didn't want her to get in trouble for being out with a man so much older than her, as she was still only sixteen. At least, that was his excuse for taking her to the park.

They would lay under the moonlit sky and make love on a blanket on the ground in the thick brush. If it was raining out, Tony would use his secondhand Oldsmobile for his trysts with Darlene. He owned a Lincoln Continental, but he didn't want to draw attention to himself by having his flashy automobile on display at the park. He said they had to be discreet. Tony took her innocence and, blinded by her youth, Darlene was an "eager" participant.

Darlene did not know it, but Tony was already spoken for. He was engaged to a young Italian woman named Carlotta, who lived in his neighborhood on the West Side of Buffalo. She was the daughter of a man who was involved with local crime syndicate activities. His name was Nunzio "Sic" Sicara. Tony ran Sic's illegal gambling operation as a bookie, and he was making a great deal of cash in that line of work. He was a gambler on many levels. He knew if his future father- in-law found out he was seeing another girl on the side, he would not only lose his lucrative job but also a body part or two. Tony was playing with fire, but he enjoyed the thrill of the risk involved.

Darlene didn't make stipulations on his time. She felt honored that such a good-looking man who seemed to have a lot of money would be interested in her. Tony told Darlene that he was a truck driver for a local cheese processing distribution center to explain his apparent wealth. Part of what he told her was true. He did drive a truck for a cheese processing center, but the large amounts of money came from his bookie activities along his route. He would make deliveries east to Rochester, Syracuse, and Albany, then go to New York City and drop cheese off at distribution facilities there. On those same trips, he was running a large illegal gambling operation from Buffalo to New York City and many places in between, all under Sic's oversight.

Tony thought of Darlene as just another notch on his belt. He was around fifteen years older than she was, and it stroked his ego that a young, beautiful girl would be so receptive to him. Darlene was very adventurous, unlike his fiancé, Carlotta, who was a prim, proper, snob, and was waiting until marriage to give up her virginity. Darlene had freely given it to him, and he found that enticing. He kept on coming back to Darlene for more.

Tony was good to Darlene in his own way. When he had a winning streak, he would surprise her with generous amounts of cash. He told her it was for being a good girl and staying true to him. Although he was engaged to Carlotta and had many more girls and women on the side, he didn't want Darlene to see anyone else. Tony told her that she was his. Darlene was naïve when it came to matters of the heart. She was swept off her feet by Tony and she was in love with him.

A couple of months went by with Darlene missing her menstrual cycle. She realized she was carrying Tony's child and had no idea what to do. She couldn't go to her parents because they would never understand; she feared that they would send her away to have the baby and she couldn't bear being away from Tony. She realized she had to tell him, but she was afraid of that, too. She wasn't sure how he would handle the news. Darlene knew that he, too, was a practicing Catholic and she hoped he would want her to have the baby. For her, having an abortion was not only illegal, but out of the question, and she hoped he also felt that way. She had heard some of her girlfriends talking about a doctor who would perform illegal abortions in downtown Buffalo. However, her religious beliefs would not allow her to do such a thing. She felt that would be committing a sin.

One evening after they finished making love in his automobile at Caz Park, Darlene told Tony she was pregnant. Darlene was dumbfounded when he grabbed her and shook her, screaming, "How could you let this happen?" Darlene couldn't believe he was putting all the blame on her. She also had never seen that side of him before, and it frightened her. Tony sat there for a couple of minutes, thinking about his situation. He couldn't let Darlene ever tell anyone that he was the father of her unborn child. If word got out, Sic would definitely take away his bookie business, if not worse. He had to put a plan in action. Although he was Catholic, he told Darlene that he would pay for her to have an abortion, and he would take her to a safe place for the procedure. Darlene could not accept that. She bolted out of the automobile and started to run home.

He quickly drove the route he knew Darlene would have to travel. He knew he could not force her to have an abortion. He caught up to her and begged her to get into his automobile. She was crying, and the cold and rain drove her back into Tony's auto. He wiped away her tears and told her that he did love her, and he would take care of everything. Tony promised her that after the baby was born, it would be taken to the Our Lady of Victory's Infant Home (known as Father Baker's) where the child would be well looked after until it could be adopted and placed in a good home. Then when Darlene was old enough in the eyes of the law, he would marry her, and they could start a family. But he also told Darlene that if she ever told anyone he was the father of the child, especially her parents, they would not be able to have a future together. Darlene promised she would keep quiet as she desperately wanted a future with Tony.

Darlene wanted to believe his empty promises. However, when she was getting ready for bed that night, she looked at herself in the mirror and saw that there were bruises on her arms. She started to think that Tony was not the man she thought he was. Unfortunately, Tony was still in her heart and his seed was growing in her belly. As the months went by, Darlene was able to disguise her evolving bump by wearing loose sweaters and pants. However, she didn't know how long she could continue to hide her secret. The only person she told about her predicament was Mabel. One night, while she and Mabel were closing up the bar, Darlene broke down and started crying. Mabel hugged her and asked her what was wrong. Darlene told her the entire story and begged it to be kept a secret from her parents. Mabel took it all in and promised no one else would ever know. She told Darlene she would need a couple of days to think of a solution to the dilemma.

Later that week, Mabel told Darlene that she would be

able to deliver the baby safely at her house. She had experience in delivering babies as a midwife, as well as some experience from nursing school. The offer came with a condition, however. Mabel would only agree to do this if Tony came to her and promised that the baby would be brought safely to Father Baker's. When Darlene told Mabel that Tony had promised to marry her when she turned 17, Mabel knew it was just his way of pacifying Darlene for the time being. She knew the promises he made to Darlene were not going to be fulfilled. He was giving himself options and trying to eliminate his problem. Mabel thought he was a narcissist and his only concern was for himself.

Unbeknownst to Darlene, Tony had recently been married to Carlotta, who kept him on a short leash. He could no longer easily sneak away. When he was finally able to see Darlene, she told him she had to talk to someone about her predicament. She didn't want to go to her parents, so she went to Mabel. Tony grew furious; he grabbed her and shook her violently, causing her head to slam against the side window of his automobile. Darlene was dazed, but this time she wasn't confused. Though she still felt she loved Tony, she realized he was too hot-tempered and volatile. She became very fearful of him, both for her own sake and for that of her unborn child.

She did her best to remain calm. What was most important was getting away from Tony, so she told him that Mabel would deliver their child at her house when the time came. However, Mabel would need to talk to Tony before she would go through with the plan. Tony thought about it for a few minutes and agreed it would be a good idea. The more he thought about it; this would be a very good idea. There would not be a birth certificate or hospital bills that would raise questions; the fewer people who knew, the better. This could be his way out.

Tony apologized to Darlene for getting upset and tried to smooth things over, but the damage was already done. She told Tony she wasn't feeling well and needed to lie down immediately. She had him drop her off close to Dolan's. It was true she wasn't feeling well, but it wasn't from the pregnancy. Darlene was sick to her stomach from Tony's shaking. She realized she could no longer continue to see him. She could handle that heartbreak. What she couldn't handle would be if he were to become so violent with her that it caused harm to her unborn child. If she continued to be with Tony, she could only see violence coming her way.

Another few weeks went by, and there was a raid at Sic's business. The police confiscated large sums of money and he was charged with forgery in the first degree, falsifying business records, and grand larceny. Sic knew he would be looking at some hard time, most likely at a prison near New York City. Therefore, he planned to move Carlotta and Tony closer to where he would be serving his time so he could still see his daughter. He also wanted to keep tabs on Tony who would still be running his illegal gambling operation, but no longer out of Buffalo.

Tony was glad to hear that he would be moving out of town. He wanted to put the entire Darlene situation behind him. In his mind, it would be like it never happened. When Darlene went into labor earlier than expected, Mabel tried to reach Tony, but he did not answer his phone. Mabel delivered Darlene's healthy baby boy. She handed the little bundle to the new mother. Darlene was crying as she held her child and looked into his beautiful little face. She couldn't get over her sadness of knowing her time with him would soon be coming to an end and wanted to treasure each moment. Mabel continued to call Tony and eventually reached him the next day. He told her he would be coming for the child later that evening.

When Tony arrived, Mabel had the baby all bundled up in a little outfit and a warm blanket to cover him. She put him into a basket she had made for transporting the child to Father Baker's. Mabel told Tony that Darlene didn't want to see him. She also made him promise he would take the baby directly to Father Baker's. Tony agreed, and he gave Mabel $200 for delivering the child. He also had an envelope of money for her to give to Darlene. Mabel refused his payment and gave back the $200. She told Tony she wanted no part of his tainted money.

She also warned Tony that if he ever tried to contact Darlene again, she would let the authorities know of his "fondness" for young girls. Tony picked up the little basket and was out the door without looking back. Unfortunately, Darlene had never told Mabel about Tony's new, violent tendencies. Had she done that, perhaps Mabel would never have given away the baby? By the time Tony walked out the door, it was already too late for the child. Since he only cared about himself, he had put together a plan for getting rid of his problem. He had heard stories about unmarried women who had given birth, throwing their newborns into the Erie Canal to avoid disgracing their families. That gave him the idea of what he was going to do. After Mabel called to tell him the child had been born, he had driven over to the Black Rock Section of Buffalo to scope out the scene. He walked to the middle of the West Avenue Bridge and leaned over to evaluate the situation below. The ice had melted in some parts, and he could see right into the water. He planned to go to Mabel's, get the child, and bring him back to the bridge that night when it was dark out.

That evening when he returned to the bridge, he had already been drinking heavily. In Tony's mind, he had to work up his nerve for what he was about to do. He convinced himself that it was a matter of life or death. He certainly wouldn't put his own life at risk, so the child had to be the one to die. He grabbed a couple of old newspapers that were in his trunk. Tony took the infant out of the basket and blanket he had been wrapped in and swaddled him in the newspapers and the black zipper bag he brought.

The child was not crying at that point, but Tony was fearful he would soon start. He couldn't take the risk of anyone hearing a child crying out, so he had to move fast. He made sure no one was around and went to the middle of the bridge. He planned to drop the infant into the open area so the child would drown. He held the bag by the strings and hurled it down from the bridge, anticipating it would go right into the water. He heard a few very short whimpers before the sound of a crack. He couldn't believe his misfortune when he looked down and saw that the bag had landed on the ice instead of going into the water. He couldn't risk staying there any longer, so he got in his automobile and raced away. He hoped when the baby's body was found, the police would assume it was a young girl trying to get rid of her "mistake." Tony had added murder onto his long list of criminal activities.

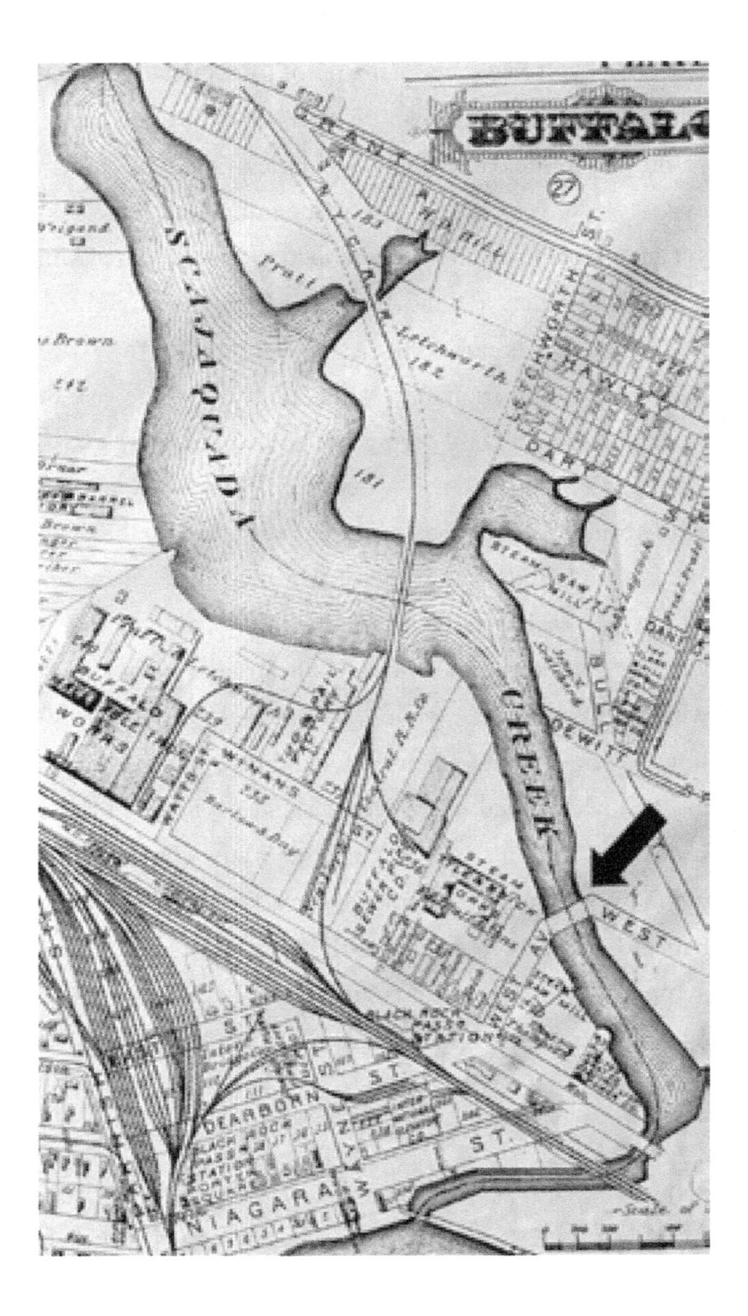
BUFFAL
SCAJAQUADA
CREEK
LETCHWORTH
DEWITT
WEST
DEARBORN
ST.
NIAGARA

One week later, Tony and Carlotta packed up their belongings and moved to Latham, NY to settle in. Sic had been sentenced to Sing Sing Prison in Ossining, New York. Sing Sing was over two hours away from where the couple was living, but they would make the drive every Sunday to see him. Tony continued running his bookie business from this new location. Sic had set him up with contacts in that area and business was never better. Tony had to give 60 percent of the money he took in to Sic, but he was smart enough to realize he should never cross his father-in- law. He was fearful of the man, and for good reason. He had heard that Sic would eliminate his problems in the same manner that Tony had recently eliminated his.

Darlene healed physically from the childbirth, but the emotional toll it took on her was something she was never able to get over. She found solace at church, and she would spend all of her free time there praying for her baby, and Tony. She couldn't help that she was still in love with him, despite all the pain that he had caused her.

Years went by and Darlene always hoped Tony would contact her, but that never happened. She eventually realized she needed to move on with her life. She went on to get her teaching degree. She loved teaching and was an incredible teacher. However, she was still not fulfilled with her life. She never spoke of what happened that fateful night when she gave her son to Tony. She prayed to God every night that her son was well cared for and loved by a good family.

In the meantime, Tony was making a great deal of money from his illegal activities. However, he could never change his ways, and he continued to seek out young girls for what he craved. Things between him and Carlotta were not going well. She had been trying to have a child, and she became frustrated she was not able to conceive. This caused problems in their marriage, but the real problem came when Tony was arrested and charged with statutory rape. He had met a young girl at a local tavern; like Darlene, this girl was just 16 years old. This time, he messed with the wrong family. The girl was the daughter of a locally prominent family with a great deal of money, and she told her father when she thought she was pregnant. It turned out she wasn't. However, her family used their power and influence to have Tony put away for the maximum time allowed by law. Since Tony's source of income stopped when he was arrested, he didn't have enough money to fight the charges or hire a good attorney.

Carlotta divorced Tony while he was in prison. He was on his own without the support of his wife or any other close family. Carlotta and Sic had completely abandoned him. The only positive thing he had going for himself was that he was not sent to Sing Sing. He would not have to worry about encountering Sic since he would be serving his time at the Clinton Correctional Facility in Dannemora, New York.

A few months into Tony's prison sentence, he was jumped by two inmates in the laundry room. He fought back but was beaten within an inch of his life. One of the inmates involved in the fight was also seriously injured. Because witnesses said Tony started the fight—and because he had a makeshift knife in his hand when the guards found him—he had additional time added onto his sentence. He would be in prison for many, many years.

After that, he constantly had to watch his back. He never realized before the extent of Sic's power or the connections he had, even in an entirely different prison. He was then living in fear. He would rarely leave his cell and he didn't socialize with any of the other inmates. He did what was required to get by, but it was a living hell for him. A couple of years went by and Tony learned that Sic had died in prison from cancer. He felt a sense of relief in hearing that news. He thought he could finally let his guard down, and not be constantly looking over his shoulder. However, the relief was short-lived. Within a week of Sic's passing, Tony found a dead bird in his cell. He would have to finish out his long prison sentence in constant fear of what Sic could still do to him, even from beyond the grave.

Tony was eventually paroled in 1992. There was nowhere he could call home in Dannemora; the only real home he had ever known was back in Buffalo. He still had a sister who lived on the West Side of Buffalo, and the parole board allowed him to move back to Buffalo to live with his ailing sister. Even though he was in his 70s when he got out of prison, he had to get a job. When he was in prison, he had worked in the kitchen as a cook and baker. This gave him the experience needed to get a job at a bakery in his sister's neighborhood. He kept a low profile and stayed out of trouble for around a year. Then, using all the money he had saved and some additional money borrowed from his sister, he was able to purchase a computer and cell phone. He couldn't believe how technology advanced while he was serving his time, and he saw an opportunity to start up his bookie activities again.

Several months into his new venture, Tony made the mistake of ripping off one of the people he was doing his illegal gambling with. Someone anonymously reported his activities to the police. He was arrested and fingerprinted, and the authorities confiscated his computer and cell phone. Tony realized there was no way out. They had him, and he would be going back to prison for violating the terms of his parole, as well as the new charges he would be facing. He was very surprised when the District Attorney's office offered him a reduced sentence—if he would identify all of the contacts in his cell phone and computer. Tony sang like a bird. He was sent back to prison on a reduced sentence and would be serving his time at Attica prison, which was less than an hour from Buffalo.

A couple of weeks into serving his time for this latest charge, Tony slipped on the floor outside of his cell on his way to work in the kitchen. There was a greasy substance on the floor, and when Tony walked into it, his feet flew out from under him and he smashed his head on the ground. He cracked open his skull and was gravely injured. He was still able to speak, but he realized he may not live very much longer. He knew his "accidental" slip on the floor was no accident. He asked for the prison priest to come and hear his confession and give him his last rites. Since he knew he was dying, he thought it would be his last attempt to make amends for his past sins.

At this point in the story, Sister Rita had to stop and compose herself. She told the detective and Michele she was almost done with her story. However, there were some things they still needed to know. She made a shaky sign of the cross and said, "Amen." She went on to explain that she had to disassociate herself from the story to get through it. Now that she had, she told them that before she joined the convent, her name was Darlene Dolan. She also said, "I am confessing to the death of my son. Although I was not the one to kill him, I am the one who set his death in motion."

Sister Rita explained that after all that had happened

with Tony Gaeta, their doomed relationship, and giving up her child, she felt she could never love or trust a man again. She decided to become a Catholic nun after getting her teaching degree in hopes of being absolved of some of her sins; she'd spent years looking for peace in her life and her soul. Saint Rita was the patroness of abused wives and heartbroken women, and since she felt she was heartbroken, she thought taking the saint's name when she joined the Sisters of Mercy was the right decision for her. She also told them the heartbreak of giving up her son didn't compare to the heartache of learning Tony Gaeta killed him. She would be haunted by that knowledge for the rest of her life.

Sister Rita ended their conversation by letting the detective and Michele know that the priest told her Tony Gaeta had told him, that he still kept tabs on her for many years. He knew she became a nun and was living in the convent on Abbott Road. That was how the priest knew how to find her. She found it upsetting and disturbing to know she was in Tony Gaeta's crosshairs for almost 50 years.

BOND OF BLUE CONNECTION

THE DETECTIVE AND Michele were reeling from this information. All of the pieces had finally fallen into place. They thanked Sister Rita for her story, knowing it was a difficult one to tell and called Butch. He agreed to meet them at a bar on Abbott Road, close to the convent. They all sat down at a table, ordered beers, and the detective and Michele filled Butch in on their visit with Sister Rita. They, too, felt they needed to start at the beginning to tell Butch the nun's story; from Darlene's tending bar at Dolan's to Antonino Gaeta's death and Sister Rita's conversion. When they were done, they couldn't tell how Butch had taken the news. He didn't talk for a few minutes, processing all he had just heard. He finally looked at both of them and said, "I never thought I would see this day. The Danny Boy case that haunted my father can finally be put to rest!"

Michele had the detective and Butch raise their glasses of beer in a toast. She simply said, "To Danny Boy, divine intervention, and karma—what goes around comes around!"

There was one last thing Butch needed to do before he could truly find peace with Danny Boy's death. Butch went home and put on his formal police uniform and the onyx ring his father had given him. Once dressed, he drove over to Holy Cross Cemetery in Lackawanna, where his father was buried. It had been raining heavily for the past several days. When he arrived at the site, he saw his father's gravestone was submerged in water. He took the single white rose he had brought with him and gently laid it down in the area identified as St. Joseph's Garden. He stepped back and softly said the words to the song "Danny Boy."

A myriad of thoughts and emotions ran through his mind about his father. Butch had always longed for a deeper, closer relationship with him. At that moment, he realized the Danny Boy case had become a way of connecting him to his father that he wasn't able to do in his father's lifetime. Butch stood at attention and saluted his father. They finally had their true *bond of blue* connection.

ST. JOSEPH
GARDEN

THE BOND OF BLUE

Written by Mary Pierre Quinn-Stanbro

The following is a poem about what my father
might have said to his father – if only he could have.

Even though you are no longer here,
My memories of you are very clear.
I still feel your presence even to this day,
And wouldn't have done it any other way.

You never got to see me **pledge to the blue.**
But it gave me peace that you knew,
I too had it in my blood to protect and serve.
We felt that is what our community deserved.

I chose to follow you into **the line of blue,**
Because of the deep respect I had for you.
But also to make a path and career of my own,
Drawing strength from the courage you had shown.

You instilled in me to be **true to the blue,**
As that was what we had in our hearts to do.
The profession we chose sometimes took its toll,
But we moved forward knowing our main goal.

This commitment to **the bond of blue,**
Can only be filled by a select few.
At times we thought the price was too high,
But we always seemed to somehow get by.

Not everyone chose **to back the blue,**
But we always remained strong and true.
With the oath we promised to keep,
Many times our emotions ran deep.

We were also bonded together with love.
And when you look down on me from above,
I hope your respect is something I have earned.
As it was from you that it was all learned.
I will forever be connected to you.
Even death cannot break **our bond of blue.**

NOTES

1. The Buffalo Courier-Express, June 2, 1945.
2. Source of article not identified, "Theft Solved by Detective on Vacation."
3. The Buffalo Courier-Express, February 24, 1946.
4. Source of article not identified, December 1, 1947.
5. The Buffalo Evening News, January 25, 1949.
6. Source and date of article not identified, "Police Rate a Well Done."
7. The Buffalo Evening News, February 5, 1950. "Liquor Retailers Honor Detectives".
8. The Buffalo Courier-Express, April 14, 1952.
9. Mary Quinn-Stanbro, Lace Around the Moon, Createspace, 2017, Pg. 10.
10. Jack Nossavage, "You know Joey Giambra, don't cha? A reflection on a Buffalo Icon. Buffalo Rising. May 22, 2020.

Mary Pierre Quinn-Stanbro

Mary Pierre Quinn-Stanbro is from Buffalo, NY, and currently resides there. She is married to Gene Stanbro and will be moving to their Gene-Pierre Vineyard in Naples, NY. She has retired from her Federal Government career where she provided 34 years of public service. Mary

Pierre is writing her sequel to *The Berry-Picker House* and *Lace Around the Moon.* It is called *The Grape Farm.* Mary Pierre has an Associate's Degree from Trocaire College and a Bachelor's Degree from Buffalo State College.

Over twenty-five years ago, she met Michele Graves while working on different community projects. She later worked with her on the BPD's Commissioner's Citizen's Advisory Group (CAG). With Michele's knowledge and contacts with the BPD, Mary Pierre asked her if she would co-write *The Bond of Blue.*

CONTACT INFORMATION:

Website: Lacearoundthemoon.com

Email Address: lacearoundthemoon@gmail.com

Michele Graves

Michele Graves most recently served as the Community Relations Consultant for the Center for Health and Social Research, SUNY College at Buffalo. She is retired as the Community Liaison for the Buffalo Police Department. Michele is on the board of Community Partners Neighbor Works America and has been affiliated with the Grant Amherst Business Association, Forest District Civic Association; Black Rock Historical Society and is a Consultant for the West Side Youth Development Coalition, SUNY Buffalo.

Michele has authored publications for the Buffalo Police Department; Buffalo State College; The International Association of Chiefs of Police; The U.S. Justice Department; The American Alliance of Museums; Black Rock Historical Society and various others. She recently co-authored a piece entitled *Confronting a Painful History - How a Museum Partnered With its Native Community to Educate the Public About an Offensive Place/ Name* (https:www.aam-us.org/ 2019/07/31 American Alliance of Museums website) and is the author of *Art as History*, included in *History Where You Least Expect it-Site Based Strategies for Teaching About the Past* (Rowman & Littlefield Publishers).

Made in the USA
-Monee, IL
14 September 2021